A gift for:

Mi Hija! Un Regalo que
Dios nos Dio Precioso

From:

Mami — Popi

You know with all your heart and soul that

not one of all the good promises the LORD

your God gave you has failed. Every promise

has been fulfilled; not one has failed.

JOSHUA 23:14

 **ZONDERVAN®**

Promises for Women
Copyright © 2006 by Zondervan

Requests for information should be addressed to:
Zondervan, Grand Rapids, Michigan 49530

ISBN 978-0-310-81008-7

Compiler: Patricia Lutherbeck in conjunction with
        Snapdragon Editorial Group, Inc.
Project Manager: Tom Dean
Design Manager: Jody Langley
Production Management: Matt Nolan
Design: Mark Veldheer
Cover Image: Stockbyte

Printed in the United States of America

11 12 13 14 • 18 17 16 15 14 13 12 11 10 9 8 7

promises
for *Women*

from the
New International Version

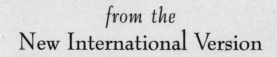

ZONDERVAN®

Introduction

God's promises—they are the birthright of the believer, an abundance of wealth for his children. Bible scholars estimate that there are more than 1,250 specific promises spelled out in God's Word, covering every aspect of our lives. What a treasure is waiting for the person who searches them out and appropriates them for her life! *Promises for Women* was created to help you do just that.

What do you need from God today? Encouragement, perhaps, or faith? Guidance or wisdom? Are you struggling with finances? integrity? commitment? contentment? Do you desire to grow spiritually, love honestly, serve selflessly? Simply find the topic that concerns you today and mine the gold of God's Word laid out for you in these pages.

As you read, remember that these are more than the hopeful insights of human wisdom. Each promise is backed by the power and authority of almighty God. Each one has been purchased by the precious blood of God's only begotten Son. And, based on eternal truth, each promise stands ready to be applied to your heart by the Holy Spirit.

Don't hesitate a moment longer. Find out what God has promised you!

⁂

The LORD is faithful to all
his promises
and loving toward all he
has made.

PSALM 145:13

Table of Contents

Table of Contents

Jesus is the yes to every promise of God.

WILLIAM BARCLAY

Acceptance

Accept one another, then, just as Christ accepted you, in order to bring praise to God.

ROMANS 15:7

Jesus said, "He who receives you receives me, and he who receives me receives the one who sent me."

MATTHEW 10:40

"You are my servant," says the LORD;
"I have chosen you and have not
rejected you."

ISAIAH 41:9

Praise be to the God and Father of our Lord Jesus Christ, who ... chose us in him before the creation of the world to be holy and blameless in his sight. In love he predestined us for adoption to sonship through Jesus Christ, in accordance with his pleasure and will.

EPHESIANS 1:3–5 TNIV

How good and pleasant it is
    when God's people live together in unity!

PSALM 133:1 TNIV

Acceptance

Jesus said, "Give to the one who asks you, and do not turn away from the one who wants to borrow from you. You have heard that it was said, 'Love your neighbor and hate your enemy.' But I tell you: Love your enemies and pray for those who persecute you."

MATTHEW 5:42–44

To love [God] with all your heart, with all your understanding and with all your strength, and to love your neighbor as yourself is more important than all burnt offerings and sacrifices.

MARK 12:33

Jesus said, "All that the Father gives me will come to me, and whoever comes to me I will never drive away."

JOHN 6:37

There is neither Jew nor Greek, slave nor free, male nor female, for you are all one in Christ Jesus.

GALATIANS 3:28

For the sake of his great name the LORD will not reject his people, because the LORD was pleased to make you his own.

1 SAMUEL 12:22

Accomplishment

I press on to take hold of that for which Christ Jesus took hold of me. I do not consider myself yet to have taken hold of it. But one thing I do: Forgetting what is behind and straining toward what is ahead, I press on toward the goal to win the prize for which God has called me heavenward in Christ Jesus. Only let us live up to what we have already attained.

PHILIPPIANS 3:12–14, 16

Commit to the LORD whatever you do,
    and your plans will succeed.

PROVERBS 16:3

A longing fulfilled is a tree of life.

PROVERBS 13:12

Whatever was to my profit, I now consider loss for the sake of Christ. What is more, I consider everything a loss compared to the surpassing greatness of knowing Christ Jesus my Lord, for whose sake I have lost all things. I consider them rubbish, that I may gain Christ and be found in him, not having a righteousness of my own that comes from the law, but that which is through faith in Christ—the righteousness that comes from God and is by faith.

PHILIPPIANS 3:7–9

Accomplishment

"Not by might nor by power, but by my Spirit," says the LORD Almighty.

ZECHARIAH 4:6

LORD, you establish peace for us;
   all that we have accomplished you have done
      for us.

ISAIAH 26:12

With your help I can advance against a troop;
   with my God I can scale a wall.

PSALM 18:29

I have fought the good fight, I have finished the race, I have kept the faith. Now there is in store for me the crown of righteousness, which the Lord, the righteous Judge, will award to me on that day—and not only me, but also to all who have longed for his appearing.

2 TIMOTHY 4:7–8

The plans of the LORD stand firm forever,
   the purposes of his heart through all generations.

PSALM 33:11

Advice & Counsel

To God belong wisdom and power;
counsel and understanding are his.

JOB 12:13

Jesus said, "The Counselor, the Holy Spirit, whom the Father will send in my name, will teach you all things and will remind you of everything I have said to you."

JOHN 14:26

I will instruct you and teach you in the way you
should go;
  I will counsel you and watch over you.

PSALM 32:8

Listen to advice and accept instruction,
  and in the end you will be wise.

PROVERBS 19:20

The way of fools seems right to them,
but the wise listen to advice.

PROVERBS 12:15 TNIV

Advice & Counsel

Wisdom is found in those who take advice.

PROVERBS 13:10

This is what the LORD says:
"Stand at the crossroads and look;
     ask for the ancient paths,
ask where the good way is, and walk in it,
     and you will find rest for your souls."

JEREMIAH 6:16

The LORD says, "Call to me and I will answer you
and tell you great and unsearchable things you do
not know."

JEREMIAH 33:3

I will praise the LORD, who counsels me;
     even at night my heart instructs me.

PSALM 16:7

Plans fail for lack of counsel,
     but with many advisers they succeed.

PROVERBS 15:22

Ambition

Be all the more eager to make your calling and election sure. For if you do these things, you will never fall, and you will receive a rich welcome into the eternal kingdom of our Lord and Savior Jesus Christ.

2 PETER 1:10–11

Christ's love compels us, because we are convinced that one died for all, and therefore all died. And he died for all, that those who live should no longer live for themselves but for him who died for them and was raised again.

2 CORINTHIANS 5:14

Make plans by seeking advice.

PROVERBS 20:18

Many are the plans in a human heart,
but it is the LORD's purpose that prevails.

PROVERBS 19:21 TNIV

Aim for perfection, listen to my appeal, be of one mind, live in peace. And the God of love and peace will be with you.

2 CORINTHIANS 13:11

Ambition

In their hearts human beings plan their course,
 but the LORD establishes their steps.

PROVERBS 16:9 TNIV

May [the LORD] give you the desire of your heart
 and make all your plans succeed.

PSALM 20:4

Make it your ambition to lead a quiet life, to mind
your own business and to work with your hands, just
as we told you, so that your daily life may win the
respect of outsiders and so that you will not be
dependent on anybody.

1 THESSALONIANS 4:11–12

The desires of the diligent are fully satisfied.

PROVERBS 13:4

Delight yourself in the LORD
 and he will give you the desires of
 your heart.

PSALM 37:4

Answered Prayer

The LORD has heard my weeping.
The LORD has heard my cry for mercy;
the LORD accepts my prayer.

PSALM 6:8–9

This is the confidence we have in approaching
God: that if we ask anything according to his will,
he hears us. And if we know that he hears us—
whatever we ask—we know that we have what we
asked of him.

1 JOHN 5:14–15

Jesus said, "Ask and it will be given to you; seek
and you will find; knock and the door will be
opened to you. For everyone who asks receives; he
who seeks finds; and to him who knocks, the door
will be opened."

MATTHEW 7:7–8

[God] will respond to the prayer of the destitute;
    he will not despise their plea.
Let this be written for a future generation,
    that a people not yet created may praise
        the LORD.

PSALM 102:17–18

Answered Prayer

Jesus said, "In that day, you will no longer ask me anything. I tell you the truth, my Father will give you whatever you ask in my name. Until now you have not asked for anything in my name. Ask and you will receive, and your joy will be complete."

JOHN 16:23–24

"They will not toil in vain
   or bear children doomed to misfortune;
for they will be a people blessed by the LORD,
   they and their descendants with them.
Before they call I will answer;
   while they are still speaking I will hear,"
                              says the LORD.

ISAIAH 65:23–24

Jesus said, "If you believe, you will receive whatever you ask for in prayer."

MATTHEW 21:22

In my distress I called to the LORD,
   and he answered me.
From the depths of the grave I called for help,
   and you listened to my cry.

JONAH 2:2

Answered Prayer

The LORD is near to all who call on him,
     to all who call on him in truth.
He fulfills the desires of those who fear him;
     he hears their cry and saves them.

PSALM 145:18–19

Jesus said, "Whatever you ask for in prayer, believe that you have received it, and it will be yours."

MARK 11:24

Call upon me in the day of trouble;
     I will deliver you, and you will honor me.

PSALM 50:15

Jesus said, "I will do whatever you ask in my name, so that the Son may bring glory to the Father. You may ask me for anything in my name, and I will do it."

JOHN 14:13–14

Jesus said, "Again, I tell you that if two of you on earth agree about anything you ask for, it will be done for you by my Father in heaven."

MATTHEW 18:19

Answered Prayer

[God] does not ignore the cry of the afflicted.

PSALM 9:12

To the LORD I cry aloud,
and he answers me from his holy hill.

PSALM 3:4

Now I know that the LORD saves his anointed;
he answers him from his holy heaven
with the saving power of his right hand.

PSALM 20:6

I call on you, O God, for you will answer me;
give ear to me and hear my prayer.

PSALM 17:6

Cast your cares on the LORD
and he will sustain you;
he will never let the righteous fall.

PSALM 55:22

Anxiety

Humble yourselves, therefore, under God's mighty hand, that he may lift you up in due time. Cast all your anxiety on him because he cares for you.

1 PETER 5:6–7

I sought the LORD, and he answered me;
he delivered me from all my fears.

PSALM 34:4

Jesus said, "Therefore I tell you, do not worry about your life, what you will eat or drink; or about your body, what you will wear. Is not life more important than food, and the body more important than clothes? Look at the birds of the air; they do not sow or reap or store away in barns, and yet your heavenly Father feeds them. Are you not much more valuable than they? Who of you by worrying can add a single hour to his life? And why do you worry about clothes? See how the lilies of the field grow. They do not labor or spin. Yet I tell you that not even Solomon in all his splendor was dressed like one of these. If that is how God clothes the grass of the field, which is here today and tomorrow is thrown into the fire, will he not much more clothe you? Therefore do not worry about tomorrow."

MATTHEW 6:25–30, 34

Anxiety

Do not be anxious about anything, but in everything, by prayer and petition, with thanksgiving, present your requests to God. And the peace of God, which transcends all understanding, will guard your hearts and your minds in Christ Jesus.

PHILIPPIANS 4:6–7

"No one will be able to stand up against you all the days of your life. As I was with Moses, so I will be with you; I will never leave you or forsake you," says the LORD.

JOSHUA 1:5

Jesus said, "Do not let your hearts be troubled. Trust in God; trust also in me."

JOHN 14:1

Anxiety weighs down the heart,
but a kind word cheers it up.

PROVERBS 12:25 TNIV

The LORD himself goes before you and will be with you; he will never leave you nor forsake you. Do not be afraid; do not be discouraged.

DEUTERONOMY 31:8

Assurance

It is God who makes both us and you stand firm in Christ. He anointed us, set his seal of ownership on us, and put his Spirit in our hearts as a deposit, guaranteeing what is to come.

2 CORINTHIANS 1:21–22

If our hearts do not condemn us, we have confidence before God and receive from him anything we ask.

1 JOHN 3:21–22

Jesus said, "I give [my sheep] eternal life, and they shall never perish; no one can snatch them out of my hand. My Father, who has given them to me, is greater than all; no one can snatch them out of my Father's hand."

JOHN 10:28–29

This is what the LORD says to you:
"Do not be afraid or discouraged. . . .
For the battle is not yours, but God's."

2 CHRONICLES 20:15

"I will search for the lost and bring back the strays. I will bind up the injured and strengthen the weak," declares the Sovereign LORD.

EZEKIEL 34:16

Assurance

Those who have served well gain an excellent standing and great assurance in their faith in Christ Jesus.

1 TIMOTHY 3:13

"Though the mountains be shaken
      and the hills be removed,
yet my unfailing love for you will not be shaken
      nor my covenant of peace be removed,"
      says the LORD, who has compassion on you.

ISAIAH 54:10

Since we have confidence to enter the Most Holy Place by the blood of Jesus . . . let us draw near to God with a sincere heart in full assurance of faith, having our hearts sprinkled to cleanse us from a guilty conscience and having our bodies washed with pure water.

HEBREWS 10:19, 22

For as high as the heavens are above the earth,
      so great is his love for those who fear him;
as far as the east is from the west,
      so far has he removed our transgressions from us.

PSALM 103:11–12

Assurance

I know whom I have believed, and am convinced that he is able to guard what I have entrusted to him for that day.

2 TIMOTHY 1:12

God is our God for ever and ever;
he will be our guide even to the end.

PSALM 48:14

I am convinced that neither death nor life, neither angels nor demons, neither the present nor the future, nor any powers, neither height nor depth, nor anything else in all creation, will be able to separate us from the love of God that is in Christ Jesus our Lord.

ROMANS 8:38–39

"I am the LORD, your God,
    who takes hold of your right hand
and says to you, Do not fear;
    I will help you," declares the LORD.

ISAIAH 41:13

[Be] confident of this, that he who began a good work in you will carry it on to completion until the day of Christ Jesus.

PHILIPPIANS 1:6

Assurance

Jesus said, "I tell you the truth, whoever hears my word and believes him who sent me has eternal life and will not be condemned; he has crossed over from death to life."

JOHN 5:24

We want each of you to show this same diligence to the very end, in order to make your hope sure. We do not want you to become lazy, but to imitate those who through faith and patience inherit what has been promised.

HEBREWS 6:11–12

We are more than conquerors through him who loved us.

ROMANS 8:37

Jesus declared, "All that the Father gives me will come to me, and whoever comes to me I will never drive away. For I have come down from heaven not to do my will but to do the will of him who sent me. And this is the will of him who sent me, that I shall lose none of all that he has given me, but raise them up at the last day."

JOHN 6:37–39

Atonement

He is the atoning sacrifice for our sins, and not only for ours but also for the sins of the whole world.

1 JOHN 2:2

Since we have now been justified by his blood, how much more shall we be saved from God's wrath through him!

ROMANS 5:9

You know that it was not with perishable things such as silver or gold that you were redeemed from the empty way of life handed down to you from your forefathers, but with the precious blood of Christ, a lamb without blemish or defect.

1 PETER 1:18–19

God presented him as a sacrifice of atonement, through faith in his blood. He did this to demonstrate his justice, because in his forbearance he had left the sins committed beforehand unpunished—he did it to demonstrate his justice at the present time, so as to be just and the one who justifies those who have faith in Jesus.

ROMANS 3:25–26

Atonement

When you were dead in your sins and in the uncircumcision of your sinful nature, God made you alive with Christ. He forgave us all our sins, having canceled the written code, with its regulations, that was against us and that stood opposed to us; he took it away, nailing it to the cross.

COLOSSIANS 2:13–14

This is love: not that we loved God, but that he loved us and sent his Son as an atoning sacrifice for our sins.

1 JOHN 4:10

God was pleased to have all his fullness dwell in him, and through him to reconcile to himself all things, whether things on earth or things in heaven, by making peace through his blood, shed on the cross.

COLOSSIANS 1:19–20

Jesus said, "This is my blood of the covenant, which is poured out for many for the forgiveness of sins."

MATTHEW 26:28

Attitude

You were taught ... to put off your old self, which is being corrupted by its deceitful desires; to be made new in the attitude of your minds; and to put on the new self, created to be like God in true righteousness and holiness.

EPHESIANS 4:22–24

Guard your heart,
  for it is the wellspring of life.

PROVERBS 4:23

Jesus said, "The greatest among you will be your servant. For whoever exalts himself will be humbled, and whoever humbles himself will be exalted."

MATTHEW 23:11–12

Since, then, you have been raised with Christ, set your hearts on things above, where Christ is seated at the right hand of God. Set your minds on things above, not on earthly things.

COLOSSIANS 3:1–2

Be imitators of God, therefore, as dearly loved children and live a life of love, just as Christ loved us and gave himself up for us as a fragrant offering and sacrifice to God.

EPHESIANS 5:1–2

Attitude

Your attitude should be the same as that of
Christ Jesus:

Who, being in very nature God,
    did not consider equality with God something
        to be grasped,
but made himself nothing,
    taking the very nature of a servant,
    being made in human likeness.
And being found in appearance as a man,
    he humbled himself and became obedient
        to death—
        even death on a cross!
Therefore God exalted him to the highest place
    and gave him the name that is above
        every name.

PHILIPPIANS 2:5–9

*Whoever claims to live in [God] must
walk as Jesus did.*

1 JOHN 2:6

Beauty

God does not judge by external appearance.

GALATIANS 2:6

[Your beauty] should be that of your inner self, the unfading beauty of a gentle and quiet spirit, which is of great worth in God's sight.

1 PETER 3:4

Charm is deceptive, and beauty is fleeting;
> but a woman who fears the LORD is to be
> > praised.
Give her the reward she has earned,
> and let her works bring her praise at the city gate.

PROVERBS 31:30–31

The LORD does not look at the things human beings look at. People look at the outward appearance, but the LORD looks at the heart.

1 SAMUEL 16:7 TNIV

Beauty

[Jesus] had no beauty or majesty to attract us to him,
  nothing in his appearance that we should
      desire him.
He was despised and rejected by men,
  a man of sorrows, and familiar with suffering.
Like one from whom men hide their faces
  he was despised, and we esteemed him not.
But he was pierced for our transgressions,
  he was crushed for our iniquities;
the punishment that brought us peace was upon him,
  and by his wounds we are healed.

ISAIAH 53:2–3, 5

Dress modestly, with decency and propriety, not with braided hair or gold or pearls or expensive clothes, but with good deeds, appropriate for women who profess to worship God.

1 TIMOTHY 2:9–10

Belief

Jesus told him, "Because you have seen me, you have believed; blessed are those who have not seen and yet have believed."

JOHN 20:29

All the prophets testify about him that everyone who believes in him receives forgiveness of sins through his name.

ACTS 10:43

Without faith it is impossible to please God, because anyone who comes to him must believe that he exists and that he rewards those who earnestly seek him.

HEBREWS 11:6

Though you have not seen [Jesus Christ], you love him; and even though you do not see him now, you believe in him and are filled with an inexpressible and glorious joy, for you are receiving the goal of your faith, the salvation of your souls.

1 PETER 1:8–9

Jesus said, "I tell you the truth, he who believes has everlasting life."

JOHN 6:47

Belief

To all who received him, to those who believed in his name, he gave the right to become children of God—children born not of natural descent, nor of human decision or a husband's will, but born of God.

JOHN 1:12–13

Believe in the Lord Jesus, and you will be saved—you and your household.

ACTS 16:31

Jesus said, "Whoever believes in [Jesus Christ] is not condemned."

JOHN 3:18

If you confess with your mouth, "Jesus is Lord," and believe in your heart that God raised him from the dead, you will be saved. For it is with your heart that you believe and are justified, and it is with your mouth that you confess and are saved.

ROMANS 10:9–10

Jesus said, "God so loved the world that he gave his one and only Son, that whoever believes in him shall not perish but have eternal life."

JOHN 3:16

Belief

From the beginning God chose you to be saved through the sanctifying work of the Spirit and through belief in the truth. He called you to this through our gospel, that you might share in the glory of our Lord Jesus Christ.

2 THESSALONIANS 2:13–14

It is written, "I believed; therefore I have spoken." With that same spirit of faith we also believe and therefore speak, because we know that the one who raised the Lord Jesus from the dead will also raise us with Jesus and present us with you in his presence.

2 CORINTHIANS 4:13–14

Jesus said to her, "I am the resurrection and the life. He who believes in me will live, even though he dies; and whoever lives and believes in me will never die."

JOHN 11:25–26

I am not ashamed, because I know whom I have believed, and am convinced that he is able to guard what I have entrusted to him for that day.

2 TIMOTHY 1:12

Belief

On the last and greatest day of the Feast, Jesus stood and said in a loud voice, "If anyone is thirsty, let him come to me and drink. Whoever believes in me, as the Scripture has said, streams of living water will flow from within him."

JOHN 7:37–38

In Scripture it says:
"See, I lay a stone in Zion,
    a chosen and precious cornerstone,
and the one who trusts in him
    will never be put to shame."

1 PETER 2:6

Jesus said, "Everything is possible for him who believes."

MARK 9:23

Jesus cried out, "Those who believe in me do not believe in me only, but in the one who sent me. When they look at me, they see the one who sent me. I have come into the world as a light, so that no one who believes in me should stay in darkness."

JOHN 12:44–46 TNIV

Bible Study

*I have hidden your word in my heart
that I might not sin against you.*

PSALM 119:11

Those who look intently into the perfect law that
gives freedom and continue in it—not forgetting
what they have heard but doing it—they will be
blessed in what they do.

JAMES 1:25 TNIV

Jesus said to them, "Others, like seed sown on good
soil, hear the word, accept it, and produce a crop—
thirty, sixty or even a hundred times what was sown."

MARK 4:20

Do your best to present yourself to God as one
approved, a workman who does not need to be
ashamed and who correctly handles the word of
truth.

2 TIMOTHY 2:15

We have the word of the prophets made more
certain, and you will do well to pay attention to it,
as to a light shining in a dark place, until the day
dawns and the morning star rises in your hearts.

2 PETER 1:19

Bible Study

All Scripture is God-breathed and is useful for teaching, rebuking, correcting and training in righteousness, so that all God's people may be thoroughly equipped for every good work.

2 TIMOTHY 3:16–17 TNIV

When your words came, I ate them;
    they were my joy and my heart's delight.

JEREMIAH 15:16

Jesus answered, "It is written: 'People do not live on bread alone, but on every word that comes from the mouth of God.'"

MATTHEW 4:4 TNIV

If you accept my words
    and store up my commands within you,
turning your ear to wisdom
    and applying your heart to understanding,
and if you call out for insight
    and cry aloud for understanding, . . .
then you will understand the fear of the LORD
    and find the knowledge of God.
For the LORD gives wisdom,
    and from his mouth come knowledge and
        understanding.

PROVERBS 2:1–3, 5–6

Blessings

Surely, O LORD, you bless the righteous;
  you surround them with your favor as with
    a shield.

PSALM 5:12

Blessed are all who fear the LORD,
  who walk in his ways.
You will eat the fruit of your labor;
  blessings and prosperity will be yours.

PSALM 128:1–2

Those who have clean hands and a pure heart,
  who do not put their trust in an idol
  or swear by a false god . . .
will receive blessing from the LORD
  and vindication from God their Savior.

PSALM 24:4–5 TNIV

The Sovereign LORD says, "I will make a covenant
of peace with them. . . . I will send down showers in
season; there will be showers of blessing. The trees of
the field will yield their fruit and the ground will
yield its crops; the people will be secure in their
land."

EZEKIEL 34:25–27

Blessings

Blessings crown the head of the righteous.

PROVERBS 10:6

Praise be to the God and Father of our Lord Jesus Christ, who has blessed us in the heavenly realms with every spiritual blessing in Christ.

EPHESIANS 1:3

Blessed is he who comes in the name of the LORD.
    From the house of the LORD we bless you.

PSALM 118:26

There is no difference between Jew and Gentile—
the same Lord is Lord of all and richly blesses all
who call on him.

ROMANS 10:12

Blessed [are those] you choose
    and bring to live in your courts!
We are filled with the good things of your house,
    of your holy temple.

PSALM 65:4

Blessings

"I will satisfy the priests with abundance,
    and my people will be filled with my bounty,"
        declares the LORD.

JEREMIAH 31:14

How great is your goodness,
    which you have stored up for those who fear you,
which you bestow in the sight of men
    on those who take refuge in you.

PSALM 31:19

*I am setting before you today a
blessing . . . if you obey the commands
of the LORD your God that I am
giving you today.*

DEUTERONOMY 11:26–27

"I will make you into a great nation
    and I will bless you;
I will make your name great,
    and you will be a blessing.
I will bless those who bless you,
    and whoever curses you I will curse;
and all peoples on earth
    will be blessed through you," said the LORD.

GENESIS 12:2–3

Blessings

Blessed is the nation whose God is the LORD,
the people he chose for his inheritance.

PSALM 33:12

Looking at his disciples, [Jesus] said:

"Blessed are you who are poor,
for yours is the kingdom of God.
Blessed are you who hunger now,
for you will be satisfied.
Blessed are you who weep now,
for you will laugh.
Blessed are you when men hate you,
when they exclude you and insult you
and reject your name as evil,
because of the Son of Man.

"Rejoice in that day and leap for joy because great is
your reward in heaven."

LUKE 6:20–23

Celebration

Praise his name with dancing
and make music to him with
tambourine and harp.
For the LORD takes delight in his people;
he crowns the humble with salvation.
Let the saints rejoice in this honor
and sing for joy on their beds.

PSALM 149:3–5

Praise the LORD.
Praise God in his sanctuary;
    praise him in his mighty heavens.
Praise him for his acts of power;
    praise him for his surpassing greatness.
Praise him with the sounding of the trumpet,
    praise him with the harp and lyre,
praise him with tambourine and dancing,
    praise him with the strings and flute,
praise him with the clash of cymbals,
    praise him with resounding cymbals.
Let everything that has breath praise the LORD.
Praise the LORD.

PSALM 150

Celebration

The LORD says,
"Be glad and rejoice forever
    in what I will create,
for I will create Jerusalem to be a delight
    and its people a joy.
I will rejoice over Jerusalem
    and take delight in my people."

ISAIAH 65:18–19

The LORD declares,
"Maidens will dance and be glad,
    young men and old as well.
I will turn their mourning into gladness;
    I will give them comfort and joy instead of
        sorrow."

JEREMIAH 31:13

I delight greatly in the LORD;
    my soul rejoices in my God.
For he has clothed me with garments of salvation
    and arrayed me in a robe of righteousness.

ISAIAH 61:10

Challenges

Since we are surrounded by such a great cloud of
witnesses, let us throw off everything that hinders
and the sin that so easily entangles, and let us run
with perseverance the race marked out for us. Let us
fix our eyes on Jesus, the author and perfecter of our
faith, who for the joy set before him endured the
cross, scorning its shame, and sat down at the right
hand of the throne of God. Consider him who
endured such opposition from sinful men, so that you
will not grow weary and lose heart.

HEBREWS 12:1–3

*I consider that our present sufferings are
not worth comparing with the glory that
will be revealed in us.*

ROMANS 8:18

For Christ's sake, I delight in weaknesses, in insults,
in hardships, in persecutions, in difficulties. For
when I am weak, then I am strong.

2 CORINTHIANS 12:10

Just as the sufferings of Christ flow over into our
lives, so also through Christ our comfort overflows.

2 CORINTHIANS 1:5

Challenges

Because the Sovereign LORD helps me,
    I will not be disgraced.
Therefore have I set my face like flint,
    and I know I will not be put to shame.

ISAIAH 50:7

[God] knows the way that I take;
    when he has tested me, I will come forth as gold.

JOB 23:10

For a little while you may have had to suffer grief in all kinds of trials. These have come so that your faith—of greater worth than gold, which perishes even though refined by fire—may be proved genuine and may result in praise, glory and honor when Jesus Christ is revealed.

1 PETER 1:6–7

[The LORD] has not despised or disdained
    the suffering of the afflicted one;
he has not hidden his face from him
    but has listened to his cry for help.

PSALM 22:24

Change

"I the LORD do not change," says the LORD
Almighty.

MALACHI 3:6

*The Father of the heavenly lights . . .
does not change like shifting shadows.*

JAMES 1:17

Be made new in the attitude of your minds.

EPHESIANS 4:23

Praise be to the name of God for ever and ever;
     wisdom and power are his.
He changes times and seasons;
     he sets up kings and deposes them.
He gives wisdom to the wise
     and knowledge to the discerning.
He reveals deep and hidden things;
     he knows what lies in darkness,
     and light dwells with him.

DANIEL 2:20–22

Forget the former things;
     do not dwell on the past.
See, I am doing a new thing!
     Now it springs up; do you not perceive it?

ISAIAH 43:18–19

Change

We eagerly await a Savior from there, the Lord Jesus Christ, who, by the power that enables him to bring everything under his control, will transform our lowly bodies so that they will be like his glorious body.

PHILIPPIANS 3:20–21

Jesus said, "I tell you the truth, unless you change and become like little children, you will never enter the kingdom of heaven."

MATTHEW 18:3

You were washed, you were sanctified, you were justified in the name of the Lord Jesus Christ and by the Spirit of our God.

1 CORINTHIANS 6:11

Do not conform any longer to the pattern of this world, but be transformed by the renewing of your mind.

ROMANS 12:2

If anyone is in Christ, he is a new creation; the old has gone, the new has come!

2 CORINTHIANS 5:17

Character

We know that suffering produces perseverance; perseverance, character; and character, hope. And hope does not disappoint us, because God has poured out his love into our hearts by the Holy Spirit, whom he has given us.

ROMANS 5:3–5

The LORD is righteous,
he loves justice;
the upright will see his face.

PSALM 11:7 TNIV

The righteous will hold to their ways,
and those with clean hands will grow stronger.

JOB 17:9

The noble make noble plans,
and by noble deeds they stand.

ISAIAH 32:8 TNIV

The highway of the upright avoids evil;
he who guards his way guards his life.

PROVERBS 16:17

Your ways are in full view of the LORD,
and he examines all your paths.

PROVERBS 5:21 TNIV

Character

Who is wise and understanding among you? Let him show it by his good life, by deeds done in the humility that comes from wisdom.

JAMES 3:13

Even in darkness light dawns for the upright,
   for those who are gracious and compassionate
      and righteous.
Good will come to those who are generous and
      lend freely,
   who conduct their affairs with justice.
Surely the righteous will never be shaken;
   they will be remembered forever.

PSALM 112:4–6 TNIV

Set an example for the believers in speech, in life, in love, in faith and in purity.

1 TIMOTHY 4:12

Remind the people to be subject to rulers and authorities, to be obedient, to be ready to do whatever is good.

TITUS 3:1

Children

All your children will be taught by the LORD,
    and great will be their peace.

ISAIAH 54:13 TNIV

Discipline your children, and they will give
        you peace;
    they will bring you the delights you desire.

PROVERBS 29:17 TNIV

[God] will love you and bless you and increase your
numbers. He will bless the fruit of your womb, the
crops of your land.

DEUTERONOMY 7:13

Children are a heritage from the LORD,
    offspring a reward from him.
Like arrows in the hands of a warrior
    are children born in one's youth.
Blessed is the man
    whose quiver is full of them.

PSALM 127:3–5 TNIV

Children

*Train a child in the way he should go,
and when he is old he will not turn
from it.*

PROVERBS 22:6

Fix these words of mine in your hearts and minds; tie them as symbols on your hands and bind them on your foreheads. Teach them to your children, talking about them when you sit at home and when you walk along the road, when you lie down and when you get up. Write them on the doorframes of your houses and on your gates, so that your days and the days of your children may be many in the land that the LORD swore to give your forefathers, as many as the days that the heavens are above the earth.

DEUTERONOMY 11:18–21

You, [O LORD] remain the same,
and your years will never end.
The children of your servants will live in your
presence;
their descendants will be established before you.

PSALM 102:28

Church

You are no longer foreigners and aliens, but fellow citizens with God's people and members of God's household, built on the foundation of the apostles and prophets, with Christ Jesus himself as the chief cornerstone. In him the whole building is joined together and rises to become a holy temple in the Lord.

EPHESIANS 2:19–21

The body is a unit, though it is made up of many parts; and though all its parts are many, they form one body. So it is with Christ. For we were all baptized by one Spirit into one body—whether Jews or Greeks, slave or free—and we were all given the one Spirit to drink.

1 CORINTHIANS 12:12–13

Just as each of us has one body with many members, and these members do not all have the same function, so in Christ we who are many form one body, and each member belongs to all the others.

ROMANS 12:4–6

Let us not give up meeting together, as some are in the habit of doing, but let us encourage one another—and all the more as you see the Day approaching.

HEBREWS 10:25

Church

Jesus replied, "Blessed are you, Simon son of Jonah, for this was not revealed to you by man, but by my Father in heaven. And I tell you that you are Peter, and on this rock I will build my church, and the gates of Hades will not overcome it."

MATTHEW 16:17–18

God's household . . . is the church of the living God, the pillar and foundation of the truth.

1 TIMOTHY 3:15

He is the head of the body, the church; he is the beginning and the firstborn from among the dead, so that in everything he might have the supremacy.

COLOSSIANS 1:18

You are the body of Christ, and each one of you is a part of it. And in the church God has appointed first of all apostles, second prophets, third teachers, then workers of miracles, also those having gifts of healing, those able to help others, those with gifts of administration, and those speaking in different kinds of tongues.

1 CORINTHIANS 12:27–28

Comfort

Praise be to the God and Father of our Lord Jesus Christ, the Father of compassion and the God of all comfort, who comforts us in all our troubles, so that we can comfort those in any trouble with the comfort we ourselves have received from God.

2 CORINTHIANS 1:3–4

The LORD is close to the brokenhearted
and saves those who are crushed in spirit.

PSALM 34:18

May your unfailing love be my comfort,
according to your promise to your servant.

PSALM 119:76

*Even though I walk
through the valley of the shadow
of death,
I will fear no evil,
for you are with me;
your rod and your staff,
they comfort me.*

PSALM 23:4

Comfort

My comfort in my suffering is this:
Your promise preserves my life.

PSALM 119:50

The LORD says,
"As a mother comforts her child,
    so will I comfort you;
    and you will be comforted over Jerusalem."

ISAIAH 66:13

The LORD is good,
    a refuge in times of trouble.
He cares for those who trust in him.

NAHUM 1:7

"I have seen their ways, but I will heal them;
    I will guide them and restore comfort to them,
    creating praise on the lips of the mourners
        in Israel.
Peace, peace, to those far and near,"
    says the LORD. "And I will heal them."

ISAIAH 57:18–19 TNIV

Comfort

[God] tends his flock like a shepherd:
He gathers the lambs in his arms
and carries them close to his heart.

ISAIAH 40:11

Comfort, comfort my people,
    says your God.
Speak tenderly to Jerusalem,
    and proclaim to her
that her hard service has been completed,
    that her sin has been paid for,
that she has received from the LORD's hand
    double for all her sins.

ISAIAH 40:1–2

Shout for joy, O heavens;
    rejoice, O earth;
    burst into song, O mountains!
For the LORD comforts his people
    and will have compassion on his afflicted ones.

ISAIAH 49:13

Comfort

[Jesus] disciples came to him, and he began to teach them, saying: . . . "Blessed are those who mourn, for they will be comforted."

MATTHEW 5:1–2, 4

The Lamb at the center of the throne will be
their shepherd;
he will lead them to springs of living water.
And God will wipe away every tear from their eyes.

REVELATION 7:17

I remember your ancient laws,
O LORD,
and I find comfort in them.

PSALM 119:52

Give me a sign of your goodness,
that my enemies may see it and be put to shame,
for you, O LORD, have helped me and
comforted me.

PSALM 86:17

Commitment

Commit your way to the LORD;
    trust in him and he will do this:
He will make your righteousness shine like the dawn,
    the justice of your cause like the noonday sun.

PSALM 37:5–6

"I will give them singleness of heart and action, so
that they will always fear me for their own good and
the good of their children after them. I will make an
everlasting covenant with them: I will never stop
doing good to them, and I will inspire them to fear
me, so that they will never turn away from me,"
declares the LORD.

JEREMIAH 32:39–40

I will establish my covenant as an everlasting
covenant between me and you and your descendants
after you for the generations to come, to be your
God and the God of your descendants after you.

GENESIS 17:7

*Commit to the LORD whatever you do,
and your plans will succeed.*

PROVERBS 16:3

Commitment

Watch out that you do not lose what you have worked for, but that you may be rewarded fully. Anyone who runs ahead and does not continue in the teaching of Christ does not have God; whoever continues in the teaching has both the Father and the Son.

2 JOHN 8–9

From everlasting to everlasting
    the LORD's love is with those who fear him,
    and his righteousness with their children's
        children—
with those who keep his covenant
    and remember to obey his precepts.

PSALM 103:17–18

Peter said to him, "We have left all we had to follow you!"

"I tell you the truth," Jesus said to them, "no one who has left home or wife or brothers or parents or children for the sake of the kingdom of God will fail to receive many times as much in this age and, in the age to come, eternal life."

LUKE 18:28–30

Commitment

The LORD said, "I will look on you with favor and make you fruitful and increase your numbers, and I will keep my covenant with you."

LEVITICUS 26:9

Jesus said, "I am coming soon. Hold on to what you have, so that no one will take your crown. Him who overcomes I will make a pillar in the temple of my God. Never again will he leave it. I will write on him the name of my God and the name of the city of my God, the new Jerusalem, which is coming down out of heaven from my God; and I will also write on him my new name."

REVELATION 3:11–12

He is the LORD our God;
>   his judgments are in all the earth.
He remembers his covenant forever,
>   the word he commanded, for a thousand
>   generations,
the covenant he made with Abraham,
>   the oath he swore to Isaac.

PSALM 105:7–9

I know whom I have believed, and am convinced that he is able to guard what I have entrusted to him for that day.

2 TIMOTHY 1:12

Commitment

If your sons keep my covenant
and the statutes I teach them,
then their sons will sit
on your throne for ever and ever.

PSALM 132:12

Test everything. Hold on to the good. Avoid every
kind of evil. May God himself, the God of peace,
sanctify you through and through. May your whole
spirit, soul and body be kept blameless at the coming
of our Lord Jesus Christ. The one who calls you is
faithful and he will do it.

1 THESSALONIANS 5:21–24

*The eyes of the LORD range throughout
the earth to strengthen those whose
hearts are fully committed to him.*

2 CHRONICLES 16:9

Those who suffer according to God's will should
commit themselves to their faithful Creator and
continue to do good.

1 PETER 4:19

Communication

From the fruit of their lips people enjoy good things.

PROVERBS 13:2 TNIV

We will no longer be infants, tossed back and forth by the waves, and blown here and there by every wind of teaching and by the cunning and craftiness of men in their deceitful scheming. Instead, speaking the truth in love, we will in all things grow up into him who is the Head, that is, Christ.

EPHESIANS 4:14–15

May the words of my mouth and the meditation of
> my heart
>> be pleasing in your sight, O LORD.

PSALM 19:14

Always be prepared to give an answer to everyone who asks you to give the reason for the hope that you have. But do this with gentleness and respect.

1 PETER 3:15

If anyone speaks, he should do it as one speaking the very words of God.

1 PETER 4:11

Communication

Confess your sins to each other and pray for each other so that you may be healed.

JAMES 5:16

Those who guard their lips preserve their lives.

PROVERBS 13:3 TNIV

From the fruit of their mouths people's stomachs
        are filled;
    with the harvest of their lips they are satisfied.

PROVERBS 18:20 TNIV

The mouths of the righteous utter wisdom,
    and their tongues speak what is just.
The law of their God is in their hearts;
    their feet do not slip.

PSALM 37:30–31 TNIV

The hearts of the wise make their mouths prudent,
    and their lips promote instruction.
Gracious words are a honeycomb,
    sweet to the soul and healing to the bones.

PROVERBS 16:23–24 TNIV

Communication

A *word aptly spoken*
  is like apples of gold in settings
    of silver.

PROVERBS 25:11

A person finds joy in giving an apt reply—
  and how good is a timely word!

PROVERBS 15:23 TNIV

A gentle answer turns away wrath,
  but a harsh word stirs up anger.
The tongue of the wise commends knowledge.

PROVERBS 15:1–2

The tongue that brings healing is a tree of life.

PROVERBS 15:4

*Let your conversation be always full of
grace, seasoned with salt, so that you
may know how to answer everyone.*

COLOSSIANS 4:6

Communication

The Sovereign LORD has given me an instructed tongue,
>   to know the word that sustains the weary.

ISAIAH 50:4

Set a guard over my mouth, O LORD;
>   *keep watch over the door of my lips.*

PSALM 141:3

He who holds his tongue is wise.
The tongue of the righteous is choice silver.

PROVERBS 10:19–20

Those who are never at fault in what they say are perfect, able to keep their whole body in check.

JAMES 3:2 TNIV

Compassion

Be kind and compassionate to one another, forgiving each other, just as in Christ God forgave you. Be imitators of God, therefore, as dearly loved children and live a life of love, just as Christ loved us and gave himself up for us as a fragrant offering and sacrifice to God.

EPHESIANS 4:32–5:2

Let your compassion come to me that I may live,
    for your law is my delight.

PSALM 119:77

The LORD is gracious and righteous;
    our God is full of compassion.
The LORD protects the simplehearted;
    when I was in great need, he saved me.

PSALM 116:5–6

*The LORD longs to be gracious to you;
    he rises to show you compassion.
For the LORD is a God of justice.
    Blessed are all who wait for him!*

ISAIAH 30:18

Compassion

You, O Lord, are a compassionate and gracious God,
    slow to anger and abounding in love and
      faithfulness.

PSALM 86:15

The LORD is good to all;
    he has compassion on all he has made.

PSALM 145:9

"Though the mountains be shaken
    and the hills be removed,
yet my unfailing love for you will not be shaken
    nor my covenant of peace be removed,"
      says the LORD, who has compassion on you.

ISAIAH 54:10

"I will betroth you to me forever;
    I will betroth you in righteousness and justice,
    in love and compassion," declares the LORD.

HOSEA 2:19

Compassion

You will again have compassion on us;
　　you will tread our sins underfoot
　　and hurl all our iniquities into the depths of
　　　　the sea.

MICAH 7:19

The LORD is gracious and compassionate.
He provides food for those who fear him;
　　he remembers his covenant forever.

PSALM 111:4–5

"They will neither hunger nor thirst,
　　nor will the desert heat or the sun beat
　　　　upon them.
He who has compassion on them will guide them
　　and lead them beside springs of water,"
　　　　says the LORD.

ISAIAH 49:10

Be sympathetic, love one another, be compassionate
and humble . . . so that you may inherit a blessing.

1 PETER 3:8–9 TNIV

Your compassion is great, O LORD;
　　preserve my life according to your laws.

PSALM 119:156

Compassion

As a father has compassion on his children,
    so the LORD has compassion on those who
        fear him.

PSALM 103:13

*The LORD your God is gracious and
compassionate. He will not turn his face
from you if you return to him.*

2 CHRONICLES 30:9

Because of the LORD's great love we are not
        consumed,
    for his compassions never fail.
They are new every morning;
    great is your faithfulness.

LAMENTATIONS 3:22–23

Even in darkness light dawns for the upright,
    for those who are gracious and compassionate
        and righteous.

PSALM 112:4 TNIV

Confidence

Blessed are those who trust in the LORD,
whose confidence is in him.

JEREMIAH 17:7 TNIV

The LORD is the stronghold of my life—
of whom shall I be afraid?
Though an army besiege me,
my heart will not fear;
though war break out against me,
even then will I be confident.

PSALM 27:1, 3

Such confidence as this is ours through Christ before God. Not that we are competent in ourselves to claim anything for ourselves, but our competence comes from God. He has made us competent.

2 CORINTHIANS 3:4–6

The LORD will be your confidence
and will keep your foot from being snared.

PROVERBS 3:26

The effect of righteousness
will be quietness and confidence forever.

ISAIAH 32:17

Confidence

This is the confidence we have in approaching God: that if we ask anything according to his will, he hears us. And if we know that he hears us— whatever we ask—we know that we have what we asked of him.

1 JOHN 5:14–15

Let us then approach the throne of grace with confidence, so that we may receive mercy and find grace to help us in our time of need.

HEBREWS 4:16

Do not throw away your confidence; it will be richly rewarded.

HEBREWS 10:35

[The Lord] said to me, "My grace is sufficient for you, for my power is made perfect in weakness." Therefore I will boast all the more gladly about my weaknesses, so that Christ's power may rest on me.

2 CORINTHIANS 12:9

Confidence

When I am afraid,
   I will trust in you.
In God, whose word I praise,
   in God I trust; I will not be afraid.
   What can mortal man do to me?

PSALM 56:3–4

I can do everything through [Christ] who gives me strength.

PHILIPPIANS 4:13

If our hearts do not condemn us, we have confidence before God and receive from him anything we ask, because we obey his commands and do what pleases him. And this is his command: to believe in the name of his Son, Jesus Christ, and to love one another as he commanded us.

1 JOHN 3:21–23

I always pray with joy ... being confident of this, that [God] who began a good work in you will carry it on to completion until the day of Christ Jesus.

PHILIPPIANS 1:4, 6

Confidence

We say with confidence, "The Lord is my helper;
I will not be afraid. What can man do to me?"

HEBREWS 13:6

In [Christ Jesus] and through faith in him we may
approach God with freedom and confidence.

EPHESIANS 3:12

When I called, you answered me;
you made me bold and stouthearted.

PSALM 138:3

We have come to share in Christ if we hold firmly
till the end the confidence we had at first.

HEBREWS 3:14

The LORD himself goes before you and will be with
you; he will never leave you nor forsake you. Do not
be afraid; do not be discouraged.

DEUTERONOMY 31:8

Conflict

Do everything without complaining and arguing, so that you may become blameless and pure, children of God without fault in a crooked and depraved generation, in which you shine like stars in the universe as you hold out the word of life.

PHILIPPIANS 2:14–16

Agree with one another so that there may be no divisions among you.

1 CORINTHIANS 1:10

There should be no division in the body, but that its parts should have equal concern for each other. If one part suffers, every part suffers with it; if one part is honored, every part rejoices with it.

1 CORINTHIANS 12:25–26

Do not be quickly provoked in your spirit.

ECCLESIASTES 7:9

Make every effort to keep the unity of the Spirit.

EPHESIANS 4:3

Conflict

He ransoms me unharmed
    from the battle waged against me,
    even though many oppose me.

PSALM 55:18

It is to one's honor to avoid strife.

PROVERBS 20:3 TNIV

Jesus ... looked toward heaven and prayed, ...
"I pray also for those who will believe in me. ...
May they be brought to complete unity to let the
world know that you sent me."

JOHN 17:1, 20, 23

Fools show their annoyance at once,
    but the prudent overlook an insult.

PROVERBS 12:16 TNIV

Hatred stirs up dissension,
    but love covers over all wrongs.

PROVERBS 10:12

Contentment

If we have food and clothing, we will be content with that.

1 TIMOTHY 6:8

Each one should retain the place in life that the Lord assigned to him and to which God has called him.

1 CORINTHIANS 7:17

Better the little that the righteous have
    than the wealth of many wicked;
for the power of the wicked will be broken,
    but the LORD upholds the righteous.

PSALM 37:16–17

Keep your lives free from the love of money and be content with what you have, because God has said, "Never will I leave you; never will I forsake you."

HEBREWS 13:5

Better a little with righteousness
    than much gain with injustice.

PROVERBS 16:8

Contentment

I have learned to be content whatever the circumstances. I know what it is to be in need, and I know what it is to have plenty. I have learned the secret of being content in any and every situation, whether well fed or hungry, whether living in plenty or in want.

PHILIPPIANS 4:11–12

Godliness with contentment is great gain.

1 TIMOTHY 6:6

Better one handful with tranquillity
*   than two handfuls with toil*
*   and chasing after the wind.*

ECCLESIASTES 4:6

The fear of the LORD leads to life:
    Then one rests content, untouched by trouble.

PROVERBS 19:23

Courage

Moses said, "Be strong and courageous. Do not be afraid or terrified ... for the LORD your God goes with you; he will never leave you nor forsake you."

DEUTERONOMY 31:6

Jesus immediately said to them: "Take courage! It is I. Don't be afraid."

MATTHEW 14:27

Act with courage, and may the LORD be with those who do well.

2 CHRONICLES 19:11

The LORD said, "Be strong and very courageous. Be careful to obey all the law my servant Moses gave you; do not turn from it to the right or to the left, that you may be successful wherever you go."

JOSHUA 1:7

Hezekiah said, "Be strong and courageous. Do not be afraid or discouraged because of the king of Assyria and the vast army with him, for there is a greater power with us than with him. With him is only the arm of flesh, but with us is the LORD our God to help us and to fight our battles."

2 CHRONICLES 32:7–8

Courage

I can do everything through [Christ] who gives me strength.

PHILIPPIANS 4:13

Be on your guard; stand firm in the faith; be courageous; be strong.

1 CORINTHIANS 16:13 TNIV

The LORD said, "Have I not commanded you? Be strong and courageous. Do not be terrified; do not be discouraged, for the LORD your God will be with you wherever you go."

JOSHUA 1:9

This is what the LORD says to you: "Do not be afraid or discouraged. . . . For the battle is not yours, but God's."

2 CHRONICLES 20:15

The LORD is my light and my salvation—
    whom shall I fear?
The LORD is the stronghold of my life—
    of whom shall I be afraid?

PSALM 27:1

Courage

Strengthen the feeble hands,
    steady the knees that give way;
say to those with fearful hearts,
    "Be strong, do not fear;
your God will come,
    he will come with vengeance;
with divine retribution
    he will come to save you."

ISAIAH 35:3–4

"When you pass through the waters,
    I will be with you;
and when you pass through the rivers,
    they will not sweep over you.
When you walk through the fire,
    you will not be burned;
    the flames will not set you ablaze.
For I am the LORD, your God,
    the Holy One of Israel, your Savior; . . .
You are precious and honored in my sight,"
    says the LORD.

ISAIAH 43:2–4

Be strong and take heart,
    all you who hope in the LORD.

PSALM 31:24

Courage

Be strong and courageous. Do not be afraid or discouraged.

1 CHRONICLES 22:13

I eagerly expect and hope that I will in no way be ashamed, but will have sufficient courage so that now as always Christ will be exalted in my body, whether by life or by death. For to me, to live is Christ and to die is gain.

PHILIPPIANS 1:20–21

I am the LORD, your God,
*   who takes hold of your right hand*
and says to you, Do not fear;
*   I will help you.*

ISAIAH 41:13

Christ is faithful as a son over God's house. And we are his house, if we hold on to our courage and the hope of which we boast.

HEBREWS 3:6

Daily Walk

This is what the LORD says:
"Stand at the crossroads and look;
    ask for the ancient paths,
ask where the good way is, and walk in it,
    and you will find rest for your souls."

JEREMIAH 6:16

Just as you received Christ Jesus as Lord, continue to live in him, rooted and built up in him, strengthened in the faith as you were taught, and overflowing with thankfulness.

COLOSSIANS 2:6–7

Since we live by the Spirit, let us keep in step with the Spirit.

GALATIANS 5:25

God did not call us to be impure, but to live a holy life.

1 THESSALONIANS 4:7

Walk in all the way that the LORD your God has commanded you, so that you may live and prosper and prolong your days in the land that you will possess.

DEUTERONOMY 5:33

Daily Walk

We pray this in order that you may live a life worthy of the Lord and may please him in every way: bearing fruit in every good work, growing in the knowledge of God.

COLOSSIANS 1:10

Be very careful, then, how you live— not as unwise but as wise.

EPHESIANS 5:15

"Those who walk righteously
     and speak what is right,
who reject gain from extortion
     and keep their hands from accepting bribes,
who stop their ears against plots of murder
     and shut their eyes against contemplating evil—
they are the ones who will dwell on the heights,
     whose refuge will be the mountain fortress.
Their bread will be supplied,
     and water will not fail them."
          says the LORD.

ISAIAH 33:15–16 TNIV

Decisions

Who has known the mind of the Lord that he may instruct him? But we have the mind of Christ.

1 CORINTHIANS 2:16

This is what the LORD Almighty says: "Give careful thought to your ways."

HAGGAI 1:5

Trust in the LORD with all your heart
  and lean not on your own understanding;
in all your ways acknowledge him,
  and he will make your paths straight.

PROVERBS 3:5–6

Jesus said, "I will ask the Father, and he will give you another Counselor to be with you forever—the Spirit of truth."

JOHN 14:16

Commit your way to the LORD;
  trust in him and he will do this:
He will make your righteousness shine like the dawn,
  the justice of your cause like the noonday sun.

PSALM 37:5–6

Decisions

The heart of the discerning acquires knowledge;
    the ears of the wise seek it out.

PROVERBS 18:15

If any of you lacks wisdom, he should ask God, who
gives generously to all without finding fault, and it
will be given to him.

JAMES 1:5

Preserve sound judgment and discernment,
    do not let them out of your sight;
they will be life for you,
    an ornament to grace your neck.
Then you will go on your way in safety,
    and your foot will not stumble.

PROVERBS 3:21–23

*I have set before you life and death,
blessings and curses. Now choose life, so
that you and your children may live.*

DEUTERONOMY 30:19

Determination

Stand firm. Let nothing move you. Always give yourselves fully to the work of the Lord, because you know that your labor in the Lord is not in vain.

1 CORINTHIANS 15:58

Be on your guard; stand firm in the faith; be courageous; be strong.

1 CORINTHIANS 16:13 TNIV

We are hard pressed on every side, but not crushed; perplexed, but not in despair; persecuted, but not abandoned; struck down, but not destroyed.

2 CORINTHIANS 4:8–9

Jesus said, "I am coming soon. Hold on to what you have, so that no one will take your crown."

REVELATION 3:11

Because the Sovereign LORD helps me,
    I will not be disgraced.
Therefore have I set my face like flint,
    and I know I will not be put to shame.

ISAIAH 50:7

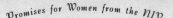

Determination

As for you, be strong and do not give up, for your work will be rewarded.

2 CHRONICLES 15:7

Let us not become weary in doing good, for at the proper time we will reap a harvest if we do not give up.

GALATIANS 6:9

[God] alone is my rock and my salvation;
   he is my fortress, I will not be shaken.

PSALM 62:6

When the storm has swept by, the wicked are gone,
   but the righteous stand firm forever.

PROVERBS 10:25

Your enemy the devil prowls around like a roaring lion looking for someone to devour. Resist him, standing firm in the faith, because you know that your brothers throughout the world are undergoing the same kind of sufferings.

1 PETER 5:8–9

Discipleship

They preached the good news in that city and won
a large number of disciples. Then they returned ...
strengthening the disciples and encouraging them to
remain true to the faith.

ACTS 14:21–22

Therefore go and make disciples of all nations,
baptizing them in the name of the Father and of the
Son and of the Holy Spirit, and teaching them to
obey everything I have commanded you.

MATTHEW 28:19–20

If they obey and serve him,
they will spend the rest of their days in prosperity
and their years in contentment.

JOB 36:11

*Jesus said, "My sheep listen to my voice;
I know them, and they follow me."*

JOHN 10:27

Jesus said, "Whoever serves me must follow me; and
where I am, my servant also will be. My Father will
honor the one who serves me."

JOHN 12:26

Discipleship

Jesus said, "I am the light of the world. Whoever follows me will never walk in darkness, but will have the light of life."

JOHN 8:12

Jesus said, "This is to my Father's glory, that you bear much fruit, showing yourselves to be my disciples."

JOHN 15:8

Jesus said, "If you hold to my teachings, you are really my disciples. Then you will know the truth, and the truth will set you free."

JOHN 8:31–32

In the presence of God and of Christ Jesus, who will judge the living and the dead, and in view of his appearing and his kingdom, I give you this charge: Preach the Word; be prepared in season and out of season; correct, rebuke and encourage—with great patience and careful instruction.

2 TIMOTHY 4:1–2

Jesus said to his disciples, "If anyone would come after me, he must deny himself and take up his cross and follow me. For whoever wants to save his life will lose it, but whoever loses his life for me will find it."

MATTHEW 16:24–25

Doubt

Jesus said, "Surely I am with you always, to the very end of the age."

MATTHEW 28:20

Are not five sparrows sold for two pennies? Yet not one of them is forgotten by God. Indeed, the very hairs of your head are all numbered. Don't be afraid; you are worth more than many sparrows.

LUKE 12:6–7

Let us hold unswervingly to the hope we profess, for he who promised is faithful.

HEBREWS 10:23

Jesus said, "Everything is possible for him who believes." Immediately the boy's father exclaimed, "I do believe; help me overcome my unbelief!"

MARK 9:23–24

The apostles said to the Lord, "Increase our faith!" He replied, "If you have faith as small as a mustard seed, you can say to this mulberry tree, 'Be uprooted and planted in the sea,' and it will obey you."

LUKE 17:5–6

Doubt

[Abraham] did not waver through unbelief regarding the promise of God, but was strengthened in his faith and gave glory to God, being fully persuaded that God had power to do what he had promised.

ROMANS 4:20–21

Be merciful to those who doubt.

JUDE 22

Jesus answered, "I tell you the truth, if anyone says to this mountain, 'Go, throw yourself into the sea,' and does not doubt in his heart but believes that what he says will happen, it will be done for him."

MARK 11:23

What if some did not have faith? Will their lack of faith nullify God's faithfulness? Not at all!

ROMANS 3:3–4

Jesus said, "Don't be afraid; just believe."

MARK 5:36

Encouragement

Why are you downcast, O my soul?
  Why so disturbed within me?
Put your hope in God,
  for I will yet praise him,
  my Savior and my God.
My soul is downcast within me;
  therefore I will remember you.

PSALM 42:5–6

*Let us not give up meeting together, as
some are in the habit of doing, but let us
encourage one another—and all the
more as you see the Day approaching.*

HEBREWS 10:25

To you, O LORD, I lift up my soul;
  in you I trust, O my God.
Do not let me be put to shame,
  nor let my enemies triumph over me.
No one whose hope is in you
  will ever be put to shame.

PSALM 25:1–3

Encouragement

You hear, O LORD, the desire of the afflicted;
you encourage them, and you listen to their cry.

PSALM 10:17

Encourage one another and build each other up, just as in fact you are doing. . . . We urge you, . . . encourage the timid, help the weak, be patient with everyone.

1 THESSALONIANS 5:11, 14

May our Lord Jesus Christ himself and God our Father, who loved us and by his grace gave us eternal encouragement and good hope, encourage your hearts and strengthen you in every good deed and word.

2 THESSALONIANS 2:16–17

Everything that was written in the past was written to teach us, so that through endurance and the encouragement of the Scriptures we might have hope.

ROMANS 15:4

Eternal Life

Now that you have been set free from sin and have become slaves to God, the benefit you reap leads to holiness, and the result is eternal life. For the wages of sin is death, but the gift of God is eternal life in Christ Jesus our Lord.

ROMANS 6:22–23

Jesus said to her, "I am the resurrection and the life. He who believes in me will live, even though he dies; and whoever lives and believes in me will never die."

JOHN 11:25–26

Jesus said to them, "I tell you the truth, unless you eat the flesh of the Son of Man and drink his blood, you have no life in you. Whoever eats my flesh and drinks my blood has eternal life, and I will raise him up at the last day."

JOHN 6:53–54

Having been justified by his grace, we might become heirs having the hope of eternal life.

TITUS 3:7

Jesus said, "This is eternal life: that they may know you, the only true God, and Jesus Christ, whom you have sent."

JOHN 17:3

Eternal Life

Jesus said, "My sheep listen to my voice; I know them, and they follow me. I give them eternal life, and they shall never perish; no one can snatch them out of my hand."

JOHN 10:27–28

Jesus said, "God so loved the world that he gave his one and only Son, that whoever believes in him shall not perish but have eternal life."

JOHN 3:16

Jesus said, "I tell you the truth, whoever hears my word and believes him who sent me has eternal life and will not be condemned; he has crossed over from death to life."

JOHN 5:24

This is the testimony: God has given us eternal life, and this life is in his Son. He who has the Son has life; he who does not have the Son of God does not have life.

1 JOHN 5:11–12

Evangelism

Jesus said, "You are the light of the world. A city on a hill cannot be hidden. Neither do people light a lamp and put it under a bowl. Instead they put it on its stand, and it gives light to everyone in the house. In the same way, let your light shine before men, that they may see your good deeds and praise your Father in heaven."

MATTHEW 5:14–16

I pray that you may be active in sharing your faith, so that you will have a full understanding of every good thing we have in Christ.

PHILEMON 6

Jesus said, "Whoever acknowledges me before men, I will also acknowledge him before my Father in heaven."

MATTHEW 10:32

Jesus said, "You will receive power when the Holy Spirit comes on you; and you will be my witnesses in Jerusalem, and in all Judea and Samaria, and to the ends of the earth."

ACTS 1:8

Evangelism

Jesus said, "All authority in heaven and on earth has been given to me. Therefore go and make disciples of all nations, baptizing them in the name of the Father and of the Son and of the Holy Spirit, and teaching them to obey everything I have commanded you. And surely I am with you always, to the very end of the age."

MATTHEW 28:18–20

Jesus said to them, "Go into all the world and preach the good news to all creation."

MARK 16:15

I am not ashamed of the gospel, because it is the power of God for the salvation of everyone who believes.

ROMANS 1:16

Jesus said, "This gospel of the kingdom will be preached in the whole world as a testimony to all nations, and then the end will come."

MATTHEW 24:14

Evangelism

Jesus said, "Peace be with you! As the Father has sent me, I am sending you."

JOHN 20:21

How beautiful on the mountains
    are the feet of those who bring good news,
who proclaim peace,
    who bring good tidings,
    who proclaim salvation,
who say to Zion,
    "Your God reigns!"

ISAIAH 52:7

Those who are wise will shine like the brightness of the heavens, and those who lead many to righteousness, like the stars for ever and ever.

DANIEL 12:3

I will perpetuate your memory through all generations;
    therefore the nations will praise you for ever
        and ever.

PSALM 45:17

Jesus said, "I tell you, whoever acknowledges me before men, the Son of Man will also acknowledge him before the angels of God."

LUKE 12:8

Evangelism

Do everything without complaining or arguing, so that you may become blameless and pure, children of God without fault in a crooked and depraved generation, in which you shine like stars in the universe as you hold out the word of life.

PHILIPPIANS 2:14–16

Give thanks to the LORD, call on his name;
    make known among the nations what he has done.
Sing to him, sing praise to him;
    tell of all his wonderful acts.

1 CHRONICLES 16:8–9

In your hearts set apart Christ as Lord. Always be prepared to give an answer to everyone who asks you to give the reason for the hope that you have. But do this with gentleness and respect.

1 PETER 3:15

Jesus said, "All men will know that you are my disciples, if you love one another."

JOHN 13:35

If anyone acknowledges that Jesus is the Son of God, God lives in him and he in God.

1 JOHN 4:15

Expectations

The LORD says,
"Those who hope in me will not be disappointed."

ISAIAH 49:23

As surely as the sun rises,
   [the LORD] will appear;
he will come to us like the winter rains,
   like the spring rains that water the earth.

HOSEA 6:3

In the morning, O LORD, you hear my voice;
   in the morning I lay my requests before you
   and wait in expectation.

PSALM 5:3

In you, [O LORD,] our ancestors put their trust;
   they trusted and you delivered them.
They cried to you and were saved;
   in you they trusted and were not disappointed.

PSALM 22:4–5 TNIV

I wait for the LORD, my soul waits,
and in his word I put my hope.

PSALM 130:5

Expectations

Wait for the LORD;
be strong and take heart
and wait for the LORD.

PSALM 27:14

I eagerly expect and hope that I will in no way be ashamed, but will have sufficient courage so that now as always Christ will be exalted in my body, whether by life or by death.

PHILIPPIANS 1:20–21

You do not lack any spiritual gift as you eagerly wait for our Lord Jesus Christ to be revealed. He will keep you strong to the end, so that you will be blameless on the day of our Lord Jesus Christ.

1 CORINTHIANS 1:7–8

Faith

Jesus said, "I tell you the truth, if you have faith as small as a mustard seed, you can say to this mountain, 'Move from here to there' and it will move. Nothing will be impossible for you."

MATTHEW 17:20

[Abraham] did not waver through unbelief regarding the promise of God, but was strengthened in his faith and gave glory to God, being fully persuaded that God had power to do what he had promised.

ROMANS 4:20–21

In the gospel a righteousness from God is revealed, a righteousness that is by faith from first to last, just as it is written: "The righteous will live by faith."

ROMANS 1:17

Since we have been justified through faith, we have peace with God through our Lord Jesus Christ, through whom we have gained access by faith into this grace in which we now stand. And we rejoice in the hope of the glory of God.

ROMANS 5:1–2

Faith is being sure of what we hope for and certain of what we do not see. This is what the ancients were commended for.

HEBREWS 11:1–2

Faith

Build yourselves up in your most holy faith and pray in the Holy Spirit. Keep yourselves in God's love as you wait for the mercy of our Lord Jesus Christ to bring you to eternal life.

JUDE 20–21

Through [Christ] you believe in God, who raised him from the dead and glorified him, and so your faith and hope are in God.

1 PETER 1:21

It is by grace you have been saved, through faith—and this not from yourselves, it is the gift of God—not by works, so that no one can boast.

EPHESIANS 2:8–9

Jesus said, "I tell you the truth, anyone who has faith in me will do what I have been doing. He will do even greater things than these, because I am going to the Father."

JOHN 14:12

Faithfulness

[God] guards the course of the just
  and protects the way of his faithful ones.

PROVERBS 2:8

*Those who plan what is good
  find love and faithfulness.*

PROVERBS 14:22

To the faithful you show yourself faithful,
  to the blameless you show yourself blameless.

2 SAMUEL 22:26

My eyes will be on the faithful in the land,
  that they may dwell with me;
he whose walk is blameless
  will minister to me.

PSALM 101:6–7

The fruit of the Spirit is love, joy, peace, patience, kindness, goodness, faithfulness, gentleness and self-control. Against such things there is no law.

GALATIANS 5:22–23

Faithfulness

These are the words of him who is the First and the Last, who died and came to life again. "I know your afflictions and your poverty—yet you are rich! . . . Be faithful, even to the point of death, and I will give you the crown of life."

REVELATION 2:8–10

Let love and faithfulness never leave you;
    bind them around your neck,
    write them on the tablet of your heart.
Then you will win favor and a good name
    in the sight of God and man.

PROVERBS 3:3–4

Love the LORD, all his saints!
    The LORD preserves the faithful,
    but the proud he pays back in full.

PSALM 31:23

The LORD loves the just
    and will not forsake his faithful ones.

PSALM 37:28

Family

How great is the love the Father has lavished on us, that we should be called children of God! And that is what we are!

1 JOHN 3:1

God sets the lonely in families.

PSALM 68:6

You did not receive a spirit that makes you a slave again to fear, but you received the Spirit of sonship. And by him we cry, "Abba, Father." The Spirit himself testifies with our spirit that we are God's children.

ROMANS 8:15–16

Children are a heritage from the LORD,
    offspring a reward from him.
Blessed is the man
    whose quiver is full of them.

PSALM 127:3, 5 TNIV

Train a child in the way he should go,
    and when he is old he will not turn from it.

PROVERBS 22:6

If you belong to Christ, then you are Abraham's seed, and heirs according to the promise.

GALATIANS 3:29

Family

Whoever loves his brother lives in the light, and there is nothing in him to make him stumble.

1 JOHN 2:10

Both the one who makes people holy and those who are made holy are of the same family. So Jesus is not ashamed to call them brothers and sisters.

HEBREWS 2:11 TNIV

Children's children are a crown to the aged,
and parents are the pride of their children.

PROVERBS 17:6

As we have opportunity, let us do good to all people, especially to those who belong to the family of believers.

GALATIANS 6:10

Children, obey your parents in the Lord, for this is right. "Honor your father and mother"—which is the first commandment with a promise—"that it may go well with you and that you may enjoy long life on the earth." Fathers, do not exasperate your children; instead, bring them up in the training and instruction of the Lord.

EPHESIANS 6:1–4

Fear

The LORD has taken away your punishment,
   he has turned back your enemy.
The LORD, the King of Israel, is with you;
   never again will you fear any harm.

ZEPHANIAH 3:15

When I am afraid,
   I will trust in you.

PSALM 56:3

Even though I walk
   through the valley of the shadow of death,
I will fear no evil,
   for you are with me;
your rod and your staff,
   they comfort me.

PSALM 23:4

The LORD is my light and my salvation—
   whom shall I fear?
The LORD is the stronghold of my life—
   of whom shall I be afraid?

PSALM 27:1–2

Fear

Jesus said, "Do not be afraid, little flock, for your Father has been pleased to give you the kingdom."

LUKE 12:32

I sought the LORD, and he answered me;
he delivered me from all my fears.

PSALM 34:4

So do not fear, for I am with you;
do not be dismayed, for I am your God.
I will strengthen you and help you;
I will uphold you with my righteous right hand.

ISAIAH 41:10

There is no fear in love. But perfect love drives out fear.

1 JOHN 4:18

Do not be afraid. Stand firm and you will see the deliverance the LORD will bring you today.

EXODUS 14:13

Fellowship

If we walk in the light, as [God] is in the light, we have fellowship with one another.

1 JOHN 1:7

Be like-minded, be sympathetic, love one another, be compassionate and humble. Do not repay evil with evil or insult with insult. On the contrary, repay evil with blessing, because to this you were called so that you may inherit a blessing.

1 PETER 3:8–9 TNIV

Let us therefore make every effort to do what leads to peace and to mutual edification.

ROMANS 14:19

Our fellowship is with the Father and with his Son, Jesus Christ.

1 JOHN 1:3

Let the word of Christ dwell in you richly as you teach and admonish one another with all wisdom, and as you sing psalms, hymns and spiritual songs with gratitude in your hearts to God.

COLOSSIANS 3:16

Fellowship

In humility consider others better than yourselves. Each of you should look not only to your own interests, but also to the interests of others.

PHILIPPIANS 2:3–4

How good and pleasant it is
    when God's people live together in unity!
It is like precious oil poured on the head,
    running down on the beard,
running down on Aaron's beard,
    down on the collar of his robe.
It is as if the dew of Hermon
    were falling on Mount Zion.
For there the LORD bestows his blessing,
    even life forevermore.

PSALM 133 TNIV

Jesus said, "Where two or three come together in my name, there am I with them."

MATTHEW 18:20

Forgiveness

Blessed are those
   whose transgressions are forgiven,
   whose sins are covered.
Blessed are those
   whose sin the LORD does not count against
      them.

PSALM 32:1–2 TNIV

When you were dead in your sins and in the uncircumcision of your sinful nature, God made you alive with Christ. He forgave us all our sins, having canceled the written code, with its regulations, that was against us and that stood opposed to us; he took it away, nailing it to the cross.

COLOSSIANS 2:13–14

If we confess our sins, he is faithful and just and will forgive us our sins and purify us from all unrighteousness.

1 JOHN 1:9

As far as the east is from the west,
   so far has he removed our transgressions from us.

PSALM 103:12

Forgiveness

Jesus said, "When you stand praying, if you hold anything against anyone, forgive him, so that your Father in heaven may forgive you your sins."

MARK 11:25

The Lord our God is merciful and forgiving.

DANIEL 9:9

Jesus said, "If you forgive others when they sin against you, your heavenly Father will also forgive you."

MATTHEW 6:14 TNIV

Bear with each other and forgive whatever grievances you may have against one another. Forgive as the Lord forgave you.

COLOSSIANS 3:13

Peter came to Jesus and asked, "Lord, how many times shall I forgive my brother when he sins against me? Up to seven times?" Jesus answered, "I tell you, not seven times, but seventy-seven times."

MATTHEW 18:21–22

Freedom

Now that you have been set free from sin and have become slaves to God, the benefit you reap leads to holiness, and the result is eternal life.

ROMANS 6:22

The LORD sets prisoners free.

PSALM 146:7

Live as free people, but do not use your freedom as a cover-up for evil; live as servants of God.

1 PETER 2:16 TNIV

We know that our old self was crucified with [Christ] so that the body of sin might be done away with, that we should no longer be slaves to sin—because anyone who has died has been freed from sin.

ROMANS 6:6–7

Through Christ Jesus the law of the Spirit of life set me free from the law of sin and death.

ROMANS 8:2

It is for freedom that Christ has set us free. Stand firm, then, and do not let yourselves be burdened again by a yoke of slavery.

GALATIANS 5:1

Freedom

Be sure of this: The wicked will not go unpunished, but those who are righteous will go free.

PROVERBS 11:21

The creation itself will be liberated from its bondage to decay and brought into the glorious freedom of the children of God.

ROMANS 8:21

The Lord is the Spirit, and where the Spirit of the Lord is, there is freedom.

2 CORINTHIANS 3:17

Jesus said, "You will know the truth, and the truth will set you free."

JOHN 8:32

You, my brothers and sisters, were called to be free. But do not use your freedom to indulge the sinful nature; rather, serve one another humbly in love.

GALATIANS 5:13 TNIV

Jesus said, "If the Son sets you free, you will be free indeed."

JOHN 8:36

Friendship

Do not forsake your friend
and the friend of your father.

PROVERBS 27:10

As iron sharpens iron,
    so one person sharpens another.

PROVERBS 27:17 TNIV

Two are better than one,
    because they have a good return for their labor:
If they fall down,
    they can help each other up.
But pity those who fall
    and have no one to help them up!
Also, if two lie down together, they will keep warm.
    But how can one keep warm alone?
Though one may be overpowered,
    two can defend themselves.
A cord of three strands is not quickly broken.

ECCLESIASTES 4:9 – 12 TNIV

Wounds from a friend can be trusted.

PROVERBS 27:6

Friendship

Be devoted to one another in brotherly love. Honor one another above yourselves.

ROMANS 12:10

A friend loves at all times,
and a brother is born for adversity.

PROVERBS 17:17

Jesus said, "Greater love has no one than this, that he lay down his life for his friends. You are my friends if you do what I command. I no longer call you servants, because a servant does not know his master's business. Instead, I have called you friends, for everything that I learned from my Father I have made known to you."

JOHN 15:13 – 15

One who has unreliable friends soon comes to ruin, but there is a friend who sticks closer than a brother.

PROVERBS 18:24 TNIV

Future

We are children of God, and what we will be has not yet been made known. But we know that when he appears, we shall be like him, for we shall see him as he is.

1 JOHN 3:2

Listen, you who say, "Today or tomorrow we will go to this or that city, spend a year there, carry on business and make money." Why, you do not even know what will happen tomorrow. What is your life? You are a mist that appears for a little while and then vanishes. Instead, you ought to say, "If it is the Lord's will, we will live and do this or that."

JAMES 4:13–15

Listen, I tell you a mystery: We will not all sleep, but we will all be changed—in a flash, in the twinkling of an eye, at the last trumpet. For the trumpet will sound, the dead will be raised imperishable, and we will be changed.

1 CORINTHIANS 15:51–52

Jesus said, "I say to all of you: In the future you will see the Son of Man sitting at the right hand of the Mighty One and coming on the clouds of heaven."

MATTHEW 26:64

Future

As it is written:
"No eye has seen,
      no ear has heard,
no mind has conceived
      what God has prepared for those who
            love him"—
but God has revealed it to us by his Spirit. The
Spirit searches all things, even the deep things
of God.

1 CORINTHIANS 2:9–10

The revelation awaits an appointed time;
      it speaks of the end
      and will not prove false.
Though it linger, wait for it;
      it will certainly come and will not delay.

HABAKKUK 2:3

*"I know the plans I have for you,"
declares the LORD, "plans to prosper
you and not to harm you, plans to give
you hope and a future."*

JEREMIAH 29:11

Generosity

We have different gifts, according to the grace given us. If a man's gift is ... contributing to the needs of others, let him give generously.

ROMANS 12:6, 8

You will be made rich in every way so that you can be generous on every occasion, and through us your generosity will result in thanksgiving to God.

2 CORINTHIANS 9:11

I was young and now I am old,
    yet I have never seen the righteous forsaken
    or their children begging bread.
They are always generous and lend freely;
    their children will be blessed.

PSALM 37:25–26

The generous will themselves be blessed,
    for they share their food with the poor.

PROVERBS 22:9 TNIV

The wicked borrow and do not repay,
    but the righteous give generously.

PSALM 37:21

Generosity

Good will come to those who are generous and
      lend freely,
   who conduct their affairs with justice.

PSALM 112:5 TNIV

A generous person will prosper;
   whoever refreshes others will be
     refreshed.

PROVERBS 11:25 TNIV

Remember this: Whoever sows sparingly will also
reap sparingly, and whoever sows generously will also
reap generously.

2 CORINTHIANS 9:6

Command them to do good, to be rich in good
deeds, and to be generous and willing to share. In
this way they will lay up treasure for themselves as a
firm foundation for the coming age, so that they may
take hold of the life that is truly life.

1 TIMOTHY 6:18–19

Gentleness

A gentle answer turns away wrath.

PROVERBS 15:1

Pursue righteousness, godliness, faith, love, endurance and gentleness. Fight the good fight of the faith.

1 TIMOTHY 6:11–12

Be completely humble and gentle; be patient, bearing with one another in love.

EPHESIANS 4:2

[Your beauty] should be that of your inner self, the unfading beauty of a gentle and quiet spirit, which is of great worth in God's sight.

1 PETER 3:4

Let your gentleness be evident to all. The Lord is near.

PHILIPPIANS 4:5

He tends his flock like a shepherd:
   He gathers the lambs in his arms
and carries them close to his heart;
   he gently leads those that have young.

ISAIAH 40:11

Gentleness

Jesus said, "Take my yoke upon you and learn from me, for I am gentle and humble in heart, and you will find rest for your souls."

MATTHEW 11:29

The meek shall inherit the land and enjoy great peace.

PSALM 37:11

As God's chosen people, holy and dearly loved, clothe yourselves with compassion, kindness, humility, gentleness and patience.

COLOSSIANS 3:12

In your hearts set apart Christ as Lord. Always be prepared to give an answer to everyone who asks you to give the reason for the hope that you have. But do this with gentleness and respect.

1 PETER 3:15–16

The fruit of the Spirit is love, joy, peace, patience, kindness, goodness, faithfulness, gentleness and self-control. Against such things there is no law.

GALATIANS 5:22–23

Gifts & Talents

We have different gifts, according to the grace given us. If a man's gift is prophesying, let him use it in proportion to his faith. If it is serving, let him serve; if it is teaching, let him teach; if it is encouraging, let him encourage; if it is contributing to the needs of others, let him give generously; if it is leadership, let him govern diligently; if it is showing mercy, let him do it cheerfully.

ROMANS 12:6–8

God's gifts and his call are irrevocable.

ROMANS 11:29

A gift opens the way for the giver
    and ushers him into the presence of the great.

PROVERBS 18:16

Every good and perfect gift is from above, coming down from the Father of the heavenly lights, who does not change like shifting shadows.

JAMES 1:17

Promises for Women from the NIV

Gifts & Talents

*Each of you has your own gift from
God; one has this gift, another has that.*

1 CORINTHIANS 7:7 TNIV

There are different kinds of gifts, but the same Spirit
distributes them. There are different kinds of service,
but the same Lord. There are different kinds of
working, but in all of them and in everyone it is the
same God at work. Now to each one the manifesta-
tion of the Spirit is given for the common good.

1 CORINTHIANS 12:4–7 TNIV

Each one should use whatever gift he has received to
serve others, faithfully administering God's grace in
its various forms. If anyone speaks, he should do it as
one speaking the very words of God. If anyone
serves, he should do it with the strength God
provides, so that in all things God may be praised
through Jesus Christ.

1 PETER 4:10–11

129

Goals

Follow the way of love and eagerly desire spiritual gifts, especially the gift of prophecy.

1 CORINTHIANS 14:1

Eagerly desire the greater gifts.

1 CORINTHIANS 12:31

Then Job replied to the LORD:
"I know that you can do all things;
no plan of yours can be thwarted."

JOB 42:1–2

Since you are eager to have spiritual gifts, try to excel in gifts that build up the church.

1 CORINTHIANS 14:12

*The LORD makes firm the steps
of those who delight in him.*

PSALM 37:23 TNIV

Make it your ambition to lead a quiet life, to mind your own business and to work with your hands, just as we told you.

1 THESSALONIANS 4:11

Goals

Jesus said, "Seek first his kingdom and his righteousness, and all these things will be given to you as well."

MATTHEW 6:33

We make it our goal to please [the Lord], whether we are at home in the body or away from it.

2 CORINTHIANS 5:9

Do you not know that in a race all the runners run, but only one gets the prize? Run in such a way as to get the prize.

1 CORINTHIANS 9:24

Forgetting what is behind and straining toward what is ahead, I press on toward the goal to win the prize for which God has called me heavenward in Christ Jesus.

PHILIPPIANS 3:13–14

Do your best to present yourself to God as one approved, a worker who does not need to be ashamed and who correctly handles the word of truth.

2 TIMOTHY 2:15 TNIV

God's Faithfulness

The LORD is faithful to all his promises
    and loving toward all he has made.

PSALM 145:13

I will sing of the LORD's great love forever;
    with my mouth I will make your faithfulness
        known through all generations.
I will declare that your love stands firm forever,
    that you established your faithfulness in heaven
        itself.

PSALM 89:1–2

God, who has called you into fellowship with his
Son Jesus Christ our Lord, is faithful.

1 CORINTHIANS 1:9

*If we confess our sins, he is faithful and
just and will forgive us our sins and
purify us from all unrighteousness.*

1 JOHN 1:9

Great is your love, higher than the heavens;
    your faithfulness reaches to the skies.

PSALM 108:4

God's Faithfulness

The LORD is good and his love endures forever;
his faithfulness continues through all
generations.

PSALM 100:5

*The word of the LORD is right and true;
he is faithful in all he does.*

PSALM 33:4

Know therefore that the LORD your God is God; he
is the faithful God, keeping his covenant of love to a
thousand generations of those who love him and
keep his commands.

DEUTERONOMY 7:9

All the ways of the LORD are loving and faithful
for those who keep the demands of his covenant.

PSALM 25:10

The Lord is faithful, and he will strengthen and
protect you from the evil one.

2 THESSALONIANS 3:3

God's Love

I pray that you, being rooted and established in love, may have power, together with all the saints, to grasp how wide and long and high and deep is the love of Christ, and to know this love that surpasses knowledge—that you may be filled to the measure of all the fullness of God.

EPHESIANS 3:17–19

Because of his great love for us, God, who is rich in mercy, made us alive with Christ even when we were dead in transgressions—it is by grace you have been saved.

EPHESIANS 2:4–5

I am convinced that neither death nor life, neither angels nor demons, neither the present nor the future, nor any powers, neither height nor depth, nor anything else in all creation, will be able to separate us from the love of God that is in Christ Jesus our Lord.

ROMANS 8:38–39

Jesus replied, "He who loves me will be loved by my Father, and I too will love him and show myself to him."

JOHN 14:23

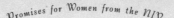

God's Love

The LORD appeared to us in the past, saying:
"I have loved you with an everlasting love;
   I have drawn you with loving-kindness."

JEREMIAH 31:3

Many are the woes of the wicked,
   but the LORD's unfailing love
   surrounds those who trust in him.

PSALM 32:10 TNIV

How great is the love the Father has lavished on us,
that we should be called children of God! And that
is what we are!

1 JOHN 3:1

As high as the heavens are above the earth,
   so great is [God's] love for those who fear him.

PSALM 103:11

God is love. Whoever lives in love lives in God,
and God in him. Love is made complete among us
so that we will have confidence on the day of
judgment, because in this world we are like him.

1 JOHN 4:16–17

God's Mercy

Because of his great love for us, God, who is rich in mercy, made us alive with Christ even when we were dead in transgressions.

EPHESIANS 2:4–5

Praise be to the God and Father of our Lord Jesus Christ! In his great mercy he has given us new birth into a living hope through the resurrection of Jesus Christ from the dead.

1 PETER 1:3

[God] saved us, not because of righteous things we had done, but because of his mercy. He saved us through the washing of rebirth and renewal by the Holy Spirit.

TITUS 3:5

I, by your great mercy,
will come into your house;
in reverence will I bow down
toward your holy temple.

PSALM 5:7

"I am merciful," declares the LORD,
"I will not be angry forever."

JEREMIAH 3:12

God's Mercy

Who is a God like you,
    who pardons sin and forgives the transgression
    of the remnant of his inheritance?
You do not stay angry forever
    but delight to show mercy.

MICAH 7:18

*[God's] mercy extends to those who fear
him, from generation to generation.*

LUKE 1:50

In [God's] love and mercy he redeemed them;
    he lifted them up and carried them
    all the days of old.

ISAIAH 63:9

Let the wicked forsake their ways
    and the unrighteous their thoughts.
Let them turn to the LORD, and he will have mercy
        on them,
    and to our God, for he will freely pardon.

ISAIAH 55:7 TNIV

God's Mercy

The Lord is full of compassion and mercy.

JAMES 5:11

Remember, O LORD, your great mercy and love,
    for they are from of old.
Remember not the sins of my youth
    and my rebellious ways;
according to your love remember me,
    for you are good, O LORD.

PSALM 25:6–7

Jesus said,
"Blessed are the merciful,
    for they will be shown mercy."

MATTHEW 5:7

[God] says to Moses, "I will have mercy on whom I have mercy, and I will have compassion on whom I have compassion." It does not, therefore, depend on man's desire or effort, but on God's mercy.

ROMANS 9:15–16

God's Mercy

Jesus said, "Be merciful just as your Father is merciful."

LUKE 6:36

I urge you, ... in view of God's mercy, to offer your bodies as living sacrifices, holy and pleasing to God—this is your spiritual act of worship.

ROMANS 12:1

The LORD your God is a merciful God; he will not abandon or destroy you or forget the covenant with your forefathers, which he confirmed to them by oath.

DEUTERONOMY 4:31

[Jesus] had to be made like his brothers in every way, in order that he might become a merciful and faithful high priest in service to God, and that he might make atonement for the sins of the people.

HEBREWS 2:17

God's Presence

You have made known to me the path of life;
   you will fill me with joy in your presence,
   with eternal pleasures at your right hand.

PSALM 16:11

Tremble, O earth, at the presence of the Lord,
   at the presence of the God of Jacob,
Who turned the rock into a pool,
   the hard rock into springs of water.

PSALM 114:7–8

This then is how we know that we belong to the truth, and how we set our hearts at rest in his presence whenever our hearts condemn us. For God is greater than our hearts, and he knows everything.

1 JOHN 3:19–20

In my integrity you uphold me
   and set me in your presence forever.

PSALM 41:12

Jesus said, "For where two or three come together in my name, there am I with them."

MATTHEW 18:20

God's Presence

Blessed are those who have learned to acclaim you,
who walk in the light of your presence, O LORD.

PSALM 89:15

*The LORD replied, "My Presence will
go with you, and I will give you rest."*

EXODUS 33:14

Where can I go from your Spirit?
Where can I flee from your presence?
If I go up to the heavens, you are there;
if I make my bed in the depths, you are there.
If I rise on the wings of the dawn
if I settle on the far side of the sea,
even there your hand will guide me,
your right hand will hold me fast.

PSALM 139:7–9

God's Will

You need to persevere so that when you have done the will of God, you will receive what he has promised.

HEBREWS 10:36

Do not conform any longer to the pattern of this world, but be transformed by the renewing of your mind. Then you will be able to test and approve what God's will is—his good, pleasing and perfect will.

ROMANS 12:2

In him we were also chosen, having been predestined according to the plan of him who works out everything in conformity with the purpose of his will, in order that we, who were the first to hope in Christ, might be for the praise of his glory.

EPHESIANS 1:11–12

The world and its desires pass away, but whoever does the will of God lives forever.

1 JOHN 2:17 TNIV

Jesus said, "My Father's will is that everyone who looks to the Son and believes in him shall have eternal life, and I will raise him up at the last day."

JOHN 6:40

God's Will

[God] made known to us the mystery of his will according to his good pleasure, which he purposed in Christ, to be put into effect when the times will have reached their fulfillment—to bring all things in heaven and on earth together under one head, even Christ.

EPHESIANS 1:9–10

God . . . listens to the godly person who does his will.

JOHN 9:31 TNIV

[God] who searches our hearts knows the mind of the Spirit, because the Spirit intercedes for the saints in accordance with God's will.

ROMANS 8:27

Jesus said, "Whoever does God's will is my brother and sister and mother."

MARK 3:35

Be joyful always; pray continually; give thanks in all circumstances, for this is God's will for you in Christ Jesus.

1 THESSALONIANS 5:16–18

God's Word

The unfolding of your words gives light;
it gives understanding to the simple.

PSALM 119:130

I will bow down toward your holy temple
and will praise your name
for your love and your faithfulness,
for you have exalted above all things
your name and your word.

PSALM 138:2

All Scripture is God-breathed and is useful for
teaching, rebuking, correcting and training in
righteousness, so that all God's people may be
thoroughly equipped for every good work.

2 TIMOTHY 3:16–17 TNIV

The word of God is living and active. Sharper than
any double-edged sword, it penetrates even to
dividing soul and spirit, joints and marrow; it judges
the thoughts and attitudes of the heart.

HEBREWS 4:12

God's Word

Jesus said, "Heaven and earth will pass away, but my words will never pass away."

MARK 13:31

Every word of God is flawless;
he is a shield to those who take refuge in him.

PROVERBS 30:5

Your word, O LORD, is eternal;
it stands firm in the heavens.

PSALM 119:89

You have been born again, not of perishable seed, but of imperishable, through the living and enduring word of God. For,

"All people are like grass,
and all their glory is like the flowers of the field;
the grass withers and the flowers fall,
but the word of the Lord endures forever."

1 PETER 1:23–25 TNIV

Goodness

Test everything. Hold on to the good.
Avoid every kind of evil.

1 THESSALONIANS 5:21–22

Trust in the LORD and do good;
    dwell in the land and enjoy safe pasture.

PSALM 37:3

Anyone who does what is good is from God.

3 JOHN 1:11

We are God's workmanship, created in Christ Jesus
to do good works, which God prepared in advance
for us to do.

EPHESIANS 2:10

I know that there is nothing better for people than
to be happy and do good while they live.

ECCLESIASTES 3:12 TNIV

How great is your goodness,
    which you have stored up for those
        who fear you.

PSALM 31:19

Goodness

Jesus said, "Let your light shine before men, that they may see your good deeds and praise your Father in heaven."

MATTHEW 5:16

As we have opportunity, let us do good to all people, especially to those who belong to the family of believers.

GALATIANS 6:10

Surely goodness and love will follow me
    all the days of my life,
and I will dwell in the house of the LORD
    forever.

PSALM 23:6

Turn from evil and do good;
    then you will dwell in the land forever.

PSALM 37:27

Do not forget to do good and to share with others, for with such sacrifices God is pleased.

HEBREWS 13:16

Grace

It is by grace you have been saved, through faith—and this not from yourselves, it is the gift of God—not by works, so that no one can boast.

EPHESIANS 2:8–10

From the fullness of his grace we have all received one blessing after another.

JOHN 1:16

Grace and peace be yours in abundance through the knowledge of God and of Jesus our Lord.

2 PETER 1:2

[God] gives us more grace. That is why Scripture says:

"God opposes the proud
    but gives grace to the humble."

JAMES 4:6

You know the grace of our Lord Jesus Christ, that though he was rich, yet for your sakes he became poor, so that you through his poverty might become rich.

2 CORINTHIANS 8:9

Grace

Let us then approach the throne of grace with confidence, so that we may receive mercy and find grace to help in time of need.

HEBREWS 4:16

[God] has saved us and called us to a holy life—not because of anything we have done but because of his own purpose and grace. This grace was given us in Christ Jesus before the beginning of time.

2 TIMOTHY 1:9

[God] gives grace to the humble.

PROVERBS 3:34

[The Lord] said to me, "My grace is sufficient for you, for my power is made perfect in weakness." Therefore I will boast all the more gladly about my weaknesses, so that Christ's power may rest on me.

2 CORINTHIANS 12:9

God is able to make all grace abound to you, so that in all things at all times, having all that you need, you will abound in every good work.

2 CORINTHIANS 9:8

Grief

The LORD is close to the brokenhearted
   and saves those who are crushed in spirit.

PSALM 34:18

When my heart was grieved
   and my spirit embittered,
I was senseless and ignorant;
   I was a brute beast before you.
Yet I am always with you;
   you hold me by my right hand.

PSALM 73:21–23

The Spirit of the Sovereign LORD ...
has sent me to bind up the brokenhearted, ...
to comfort all who mourn,
   and provide for those who grieve in Zion ...
the oil of gladness
   instead of mourning,
and a garment of praise
   instead of a spirit of despair.

ISAIAH 61:1–3

Grief

Jesus said, "I tell you the truth, you will weep and mourn while the world rejoices. You will grieve, but your grief will turn to joy."

JOHN 16:20

The ransomed of the LORD will return.
They will enter Zion with singing;
    everlasting joy will crown their heads.
Gladness and joy will overtake them,
    and sorrow and sighing will flee away.

ISAIAH 35:10

Remember your word to your servant,
    for you have given me hope.
My comfort in my suffering is this:
    Your promise preserves my life.

PSALM 119:49–50

Jesus said,
"Blessed are those who mourn,
    for they will be comforted."

MATTHEW 5:4

Guidance

If I rise on the wings of the dawn,
    if I settle on the far side of the sea,
even there your hand will guide me,
    your right hand will hold me fast.

PSALM 139:9–10

*I will instruct you and teach you
    in the way you should go;
I will counsel you and watch over you.*

PSALM 32:8

The LORD is my shepherd, I shall not be in want.
    He makes me lie down in green pastures,
he leads me beside quiet waters,
    he restores my soul.
He guides me in paths of righteousness
    for his name's sake.

PSALM 23:1–3

The LORD will guide you always;
    he will satisfy your needs in a sun-scorched land
    and will strengthen your frame.
You will be like a well-watered garden,
    like a spring whose waters never fail.

ISAIAH 58:11

Guidance

Jesus said, "When he, the Spirit of truth, comes, he will guide you into all truth. He will not speak on his own; he will speak only what he hears, and he will tell you what is yet to come."

JOHN 16:13

Whether you turn to the right or to the left, your ears will hear a voice behind you, saying, "This is the way; walk in it."

ISAIAH 30:21

Good and upright is the LORD;
therefore he instructs sinners in
his ways.
He guides the humble in what is right
and teaches them his way.

PSALM 25:8–9

Guilt

Jesus said, "In the same way, I tell you, there is rejoicing in the presence of the angels of God over one sinner who repents."

LUKE 15:10

Turn from evil and do good;
then you will dwell in the land forever.

PSALM 37:27

Praise the LORD.
He provided redemption for his people;
he ordained his covenant forever—
holy and awesome is his name.

PSALM 111:1, 9

Then I acknowledged my sin to you
and did not cover up my iniquity.
I said, "I will confess
my transgressions to the LORD"—
and you forgave
the guilt of my sin.

PSALM 32:5

If the wicked turn away from all the sins they have committed and keep all my decrees and do what is just and right, they will surely live; they will not die.

EZEKIEL 18:21 TNIV

Guilt

Repent, then, and turn to God, so that your sins may be wiped out, that times of refreshing may come from the Lord, and that he may send the Christ, who has been appointed for you—even Jesus.

ACTS 3:19–20

My dear children, I write this to you so that you will not sin. But if anybody does sin, we have one who speaks to the Father in our defense—Jesus Christ, the Righteous One.

1 JOHN 2:1

Let us draw near to God with a sincere heart in full assurance of faith, having our hearts sprinkled to cleanse us from a guilty conscience and having our bodies washed with pure water.

HEBREWS 10:22

Godly sorrow brings repentance that leads to salvation and leaves no regret.

2 CORINTHIANS 7:10

Guilt

There is now no condemnation for those who are in Christ Jesus, because through Christ Jesus the law of the Spirit of life set me free from the law of sin and death. For what the law was powerless to do in that it was weakened by the sinful nature, God did by sending his own Son in the likeness of sinful man to be a sin offering.

ROMANS 8:1–3

Create in me a pure heart, O God,
and renew a steadfast spirit within me.

PSALM 51:10

This is what the LORD says, "I will cleanse them from all the sin they have committed against me and will forgive all their sins of rebellion against me."

JEREMIAH 33:8

Christ loved the church and gave himself up for her to make her holy, cleansing her by the washing with water through the word, and to present her to himself as a radiant church, without stain or wrinkle or any other blemish, but holy and blameless.

EPHESIANS 5:25–27

Guilt

Put your hope in the LORD,
*   for with the LORD is unfailing love*
*   and with him is full redemption.*

PSALM 130:7

I have swept away your offenses like a cloud,
    your sins like the morning mist.
Return to me,
    for I have redeemed you.

ISAIAH 44:22

[God] has rescued us from the dominion of darkness
and brought us into the kingdom of the Son he
loves, in whom we have redemption, the forgiveness
of sins.

COLOSSIANS 1:13–14

It was not with perishable things such as silver or
gold that you were redeemed from the empty way of
life handed down to you from your forefathers, but
with the precious blood of Christ, a lamb without
blemish or defect.

1 PETER 1:18–21

Happiness

I commend the enjoyment of life, because there is
nothing better for people under the sun than to eat
and drink and be glad. Then joy will accompany
them in their toil all the days of the life God has
given them under the sun.

ECCLESIASTES 8:15 TNIV

When times are good, be happy;
    but when times are bad, consider:
God has made the one
    as well as the other.

ECCLESIASTES 7:14

Be glad, O people of Zion,
    rejoice in the LORD your God,
for he has given you
    the autumn rains in righteousness.
He sends you abundant showers,
    both autumn and spring rains, as before.

JOEL 2:23

Happiness

To the person who pleases him, God gives wisdom, knowledge and happiness.

ECCLESIASTES 2:26 TNIV

May the righteous be glad
and rejoice before God;
may they be happy and joyful.

PSALM 68:3

I know that there is nothing better for people than to be happy and to do good while they live.

ECCLESIASTES 3:12 TNIV

When God gives people wealth and possessions, and the ability to enjoy them, to accept their lot and be happy in their toil—this is a gift of God.

ECCLESIASTES 5:19 TNIV

A happy heart makes the face cheerful,
but heartache crushes the spirit.

PROVERBS 15:13

Health & Healing

A heart at peace gives life to the body.

PROVERBS 14:30

This is what the LORD says, "I will heal my people and will let them enjoy abundant peace and security."

JEREMIAH 33:6

O LORD my God, I called to you for help
 and you healed me.
O LORD, you brought me up from the grave;
 you spared me from going down into the pit.

PSALM 30:2–3

"I will restore you to health
 and heal your wounds," declares the LORD.

JEREMIAH 30:17

I am the LORD, who heals you.

EXODUS 15:26

A cheerful look brings joy to the heart,
 and good news gives health to the bones.

PROVERBS 15:30

Health & Healing

Do not be wise in your own eyes;
    fear the LORD and shun evil.
This will bring health to your body
    and nourishment to your bones.

PROVERBS 3:7–8

The prayer offered in faith will make the sick person
well; the Lord will raise him up.

JAMES 5:15

Praise the LORD, O my soul,
    and forget not all his benefits—
who forgives all your sins
    and heals all your diseases.

PSALM 103:2–3

He himself bore our sins in his body on the tree, so
that we might die to sins and live for righteousness;
by his wounds you have been healed.

1 PETER 2:24

Heaven

The Lord himself will come down from heaven, with a loud command, with the voice of the archangel and with the trumpet of God, and the dead in Christ will rise first. After that, we who are still alive and are left will be caught up together with them in the clouds to meet the Lord in the air. And so we will be with the Lord forever.

1 THESSALONIANS 4:16–17

If the earthly tent we live in is destroyed, we have a building from God, an eternal house in heaven, not built by human hands.

2 CORINTHIANS 5:1

Never again will they hunger;
    never again will they thirst.
The sun will not bear upon them,
    nor any scorching heat.
For the Lamb at the center of the throne will be
        their shepherd;
    he will lead them to springs of living water.
And God will wipe away every tear from their eyes.

REVELATION 7:16–17

Nothing impure will ever enter it, nor will anyone who does what is shameful or deceitful, but only those whose names are written in the Lamb's book of life.

REVELATION 21:27

Heaven

*Surely goodness and love will follow me
    all the days of my life,
and I will dwell in the house of the LORD
    forever.*

PSALM 23:6

Jesus said, "In my Father's house are many rooms; if it were not so, I would have told you. I am going there to prepare a place for you. And if I go and prepare a place for you, I will come back and take you to be with me that you also may be where I am."

JOHN 14:2–3

The throne of God and of the Lamb will be in the city, and his servants will serve him. They will see his face, and his name will be on their foreheads. There will be no more night. They will not need the light of a lamp or the light of the sun, for the Lord God will give them light. And they will reign for ever and ever.

REVELATION 22:3–5

God himself will be with them and be their God. He will wipe every tear from their eyes. There will be no more death or mourning or crying or pain, for the old order of things has passed away.

REVELATION 21:3–4   163

Help

God is our refuge and strength,
an ever present help in trouble.

PSALM 46:1

[God] will deliver the needy who cry out,
the afflicted who have no one to help.

PSALM 72:12

O God, ... the victim commits himself to you;
you are the helper of the fatherless.

PSALM 10:14

We wait in hope for the LORD;
he is our help and our shield.

PSALM 33:20

The Spirit helps us in our weakness. We do not
know what we ought to pray for, but the Spirit
himself intercedes for us with groans that words
cannot express.

ROMANS 8:26

Help

So we say with confidence,

"The Lord is my helper; I will not be afraid.
   What can man do to me?"

HEBREWS 13:6

Because he himself suffered when he was tempted,
he is able to help those who are being tempted.

HEBREWS 2:18

It is the Sovereign LORD who helps me.
   Who is he that will condemn me?
They will all wear out like a garment;
   the moths will eat them up.

ISAIAH 50:9

The LORD is my strength and my shield;
   my heart trusts in him, and I am helped.
My heart leaps for joy
   and I will give thanks to him in song.

PSALM 28:7

Holy Spirit

Repent and be baptized, every one of you, in the name of Jesus Christ for the forgiveness of your sins. And you will receive the gift of the Holy Spirit. The promise is for you and your children and for all who are far off—for all whom the Lord our God will call.

ACTS 2:38–39

"I will pour out my Spirit on all people.
Your sons and daughters will prophesy,
 your old men will dream dreams,
 your young men will see visions.
Even on my servants, both men and women,
 I will pour out my Spirit," says the LORD.

JOEL 2:28–29

You also were included in Christ when you heard the word of truth, the gospel of your salvation. Having believed, you were marked in him with a seal, the promised Holy Spirit, who is a deposit guaranteeing our inheritance until the redemption of those who are God's possession.

EPHESIANS 1:13–14

We have not received the spirit of the world but the Spirit who is from God, that we may understand what God has freely given us.

1 CORINTHIANS 2:12

Holy Spirit

Do not believe every spirit, but test the spirits to see whether they are from God.... This is how you can recognize the Spirit of God: Every spirit that acknowledges that Jesus Christ has come in the flesh is from God.

1 JOHN 4:1–2

The Lord is the Spirit, and where the Spirit of the Lord is, there is freedom.

2 CORINTHIANS 3:17

Jesus said, "I will ask the Father and he will give you another Counselor to be with you forever—the Spirit of truth. The world cannot accept him, because it neither sees him nor knows him. But you know him for he lives with you and will be in you."

JOHN 14:16–18

If the Spirit of him who raised Jesus from the dead is living in you, he who raised Christ from the dead will also give life to your mortal bodies through his Spirit, who lives in you.

ROMANS 8:11

Honesty

Whatever is true, whatever is noble, whatever is right, whatever is pure, whatever is lovely, whatever is admirable—if anything is excellent or praiseworthy—think about such things.

PHILIPPIANS 4:8

An honest answer
    is like a kiss on the lips.

PROVERBS 24:26

"Those who walk righteously
    and speak what is right,
who reject gain from extortion
    and keep their hands from accepting bribes,
who stop their ears against plots of murder
    and shut their eyes against contemplating evil—
they are the ones who will dwell on the heights,
    whose refuge will be the mountain fortress.
Their bread will be supplied,
    and water will not fail them."
        says the LORD.

ISAIAH 33:15–16 TNIV

Honesty

Kings take pleasure in honest lips;
   they value persons who speak what is right.

PROVERBS 16:13 TNIV

Whoever of you loves life
   and desires to see many good days,
keep your tongue from evil
   and your lips from speaking lies.

PSALM 34:12–13

A truthful witness gives honest testimony.

PROVERBS 12:17

The LORD detests lying lips,
   but he delights in people who are trustworthy.

PROVERBS 12:22 TNIV

Truthful lips endure forever.

PROVERBS 12:19

Hope

Blessed is he whose help is the God of Jacob,
    whose hope is in the LORD his God,
the Maker of heaven and earth,
    the sea, and everything in them
    the LORD, who remains faithful forever.

PSALM 146:5–6

We have put our hope in the living God, who is the Savior of all people, and especially of those who believe.

1 TIMOTHY 4:10 TNIV

We rejoice in the hope of the glory of God. Not only so, but we also rejoice in our sufferings, because we know that suffering produces perseverance; perseverance, character; and character, hope. And hope does not disappoint us, because God has poured out his love into our hearts by the Holy Spirit, whom he has given us.

ROMANS 5:2–5

Know also that wisdom is sweet to your soul;
    if you find it, there is a future hope for you,
    and your hope will not be cut off.

PROVERBS 24:14

Hope

No one whose hope is in you
will ever be put to shame.

PSALM 25:3

The eyes of the LORD are on those who fear him,
on those whose hope is in his unfailing love.

PSALM 33:18

May the God of hope fill you with all joy and peace
as you trust in him, so that you may overflow with
hope by the power of the Holy Spirit.

ROMANS 15:13

Set your hope fully on the grace to be given you
when Jesus Christ is revealed.

1 PETER 1:13

Those who hope in the LORD
will renew their strength.
They will soar on wings like eagles;
they will run and not grow weary,
they will walk and not be faint.

ISAIAH 40:31

Humility

Pride brings a person low,
   but the lowly in spirit gain honor.

PROVERBS 29:23 TNIV

You, [O LORD], save the humble,
   but your eyes are on the haughty to bring
      them low.

2 SAMUEL 22:28

Humility and the fear of the LORD
   bring wealth and honor and life.

PROVERBS 22:4

Clothe yourselves with humility toward one
another, because, "God opposes the proud but gives
grace to the humble." Humble yourselves, therefore,
under God's mighty hand, that he may lift you up in
due time.

1 PETER 5:5–6

Humble yourselves before the Lord,
and he will lift you up.

JAMES 4:10

Humility

The LORD takes delight in his people;
  he crowns the humble with salvation.

PSALM 149:4

*The LORD sustains the humble
  but casts the wicked to the ground.*

PSALM 147:6

He guides the humble in what is right
  and teaches them his way.

PSALM 25:9

Jesus said, "The greatest among you will be your
servant. For whoever exalts himself will be humbled,
and whoever humbles himself will be exalted."

MATTHEW 23:11–12

Do not think of yourself more highly than you
ought, but rather think of yourself with sober
judgment, in accordance with the measure of faith
God has given you.

ROMANS 12:3

Identity

You also were included in Christ when you heard the word of truth, the gospel of your salvation. Having believed, you were marked in him with a seal, the promised Holy Spirit, who is a deposit guaranteeing our inheritance until the redemption of those who are God's possession.

EPHESIANS 1:13–14

"Before I formed you in the womb I knew you,
before you were born I set you apart,"
says the LORD.

JEREMIAH 1:5

Come, let us bow down in worship,
let us kneel before the LORD our Maker;
for he is our God
and we are the people of his pasture,
the flock under his care.

PSALM 95:6–7

Know that the LORD is God.
It is he who made us, and we are his;
We are his people, the sheep of his pasture.

PSALM 100:3

Identity

You are a chosen people, a royal priesthood, a holy nation, a people belonging to God, that you may declare the praises of him who called you out of darkness into his wonderful light.

1 PETER 2:9

We are God's workmanship, created in Christ Jesus to do good works, which God prepared in advance for us to do.

EPHESIANS 2:10

Now, this is what the LORD says ...
"Fear not, for I have redeemed you;
I have summoned you by name; you are mine."

ISAIAH 43:1

Integrity

He holds victory in store for the upright,
  he is a shield to those whose walk is blameless,
For he guards the course of the just
  and protects the way of his faithful ones.

PROVERBS 2:7–8

Those who walk uprightly enter into peace.

ISAIAH 57:2

In my integrity you uphold me
  and set me in your presence forever.

PSALM 41:12

The righteous lead blameless lives;
  blessed are their children after them.

PROVERBS 20:7 TNIV

The LORD God is a sun and shield;
  the LORD bestows favor and honor;
no good thing does he withhold
  from those whose walk is blameless.

PSALM 84:11

Integrity

The integrity of the upright guides them.

PROVERBS 11:3

Whoever walks in integrity walks securely.

PROVERBS 10:9 TNIV

Jesus said, "Whoever can be trusted with very little can also be trusted with much, and whoever is dishonest with very little will also be dishonest with much."

LUKE 16:10

I know, my God, that you test the heart and are pleased with integrity.

1 CHRONICLES 29:17

Righteousness guards the person of integrity.

PROVERBS 13:6 TNIV

Jesus Christ

Our citizenship is in heaven. And we eagerly await a Savior from there, the Lord Jesus Christ, who, by the power that enables him to bring everything under his control, will transform our lowly bodies so that they will be like his glorious body.

PHILIPPIANS 3:20–21

Jesus Christ is the same yesterday and today and forever.

HEBREWS 13:8

Christ is the mediator of a new covenant, that those who are called may receive the promised eternal inheritance—now that he has died as a ransom to set them free from the sins committed under the first covenant.

HEBREWS 9:15

[Jesus Christ] is the atoning sacrifice for our sins, and not only for ours but also for the sins of the whole world.

1 JOHN 2:2

In Christ all the fullness of the Deity lives in bodily form, and you have been given fullness in Christ, who is the head over every power and authority.

COLOSSIANS 2:9–10

Jesus Christ

The angel said to her, ... "Mary, you have found favor with God. You will be with child and give birth to a son, and you are to give him the name Jesus. He will be great and will be called the Son of the Most High. ... "How will this be," Mary asked the angel, "since I am a virgin?" The angel answered, "The Holy Spirit will come upon you, and the power of the Most High will overshadow you. So the holy one to be born will be called the Son of God."

LUKE 1:30–32, 34–35

Therefore God exalted him to the highest place
    and gave him the name that is above every
        name,
that at the name of Jesus every knee should bow,
    in heaven and on earth and under the earth,
and every tongue confess that Jesus Christ is Lord,
    to the glory of God the Father.

PHILIPPIANS 2:9–11

*This is how we know what love is:
Jesus Christ laid down his life for us.*

1 JOHN 3:16

179

Joy

The joy of the LORD is your strength.

NEHEMIAH 8:10

You have made known to me the path of life;
  you will fill me with joy in your presence,
  with eternal pleasures at your right hand.

PSALM 16:11

Though you have not seen Jesus, you love him; and
even though you do not see him now, you believe in
him and are filled with an inexpressible and glorious
joy, for you are receiving the goal of your faith, the
salvation of your souls.

1 PETER 1:8–9

Let all who take refuge in you be glad;
  let them ever sing for joy.

PSALM 5:11

The precepts of the LORD are right,
giving joy to the heart.

PSALM 19:8

Consider it pure joy ... whenever you face trials of
many kinds, because you know that the testing of
your faith develops perseverance.

JAMES 1:2–3

Joy

The LORD your God will bless you in all your harvest and in all the work of your hands, and your joy will be complete.

DEUTERONOMY 16:15

Rejoice in the Lord always. I will say it again: Rejoice!

PHILIPPIANS 4:4

You turned my wailing into dancing;
> you removed my sackcloth and clothed me
>> with joy,
that my heart may sing to you and not be silent.
> O LORD my God, I will give thanks forever.

PSALM 30:11–12

Those who sow in tears
> *will reap with songs of joy.*

PSALM 126:5

You make me glad by your deeds, O LORD;
> I sing for joy at the works of your hands.

PSALM 92:4

Joy

Tremble before him, all the earth!
>The world is firmly established; it cannot be
>>moved.
Let the heavens rejoice, let the earth be glad;
>let them say among the nations, "The LORD
>>reigns!"
Let the sea resound, and all that is in it;
>let the fields be jubilant, and everything in
>>them!
Then the trees of the forest will sing,
>they will sing for joy before the LORD,
>for he comes to judge the earth.

1 CHRONICLES 16:30–33

Light is shed upon the righteous
and joy on the upright in heart.

PSALM 97:11

Your statutes are my heritage forever;
>they are the joy of my heart.

PSALM 119:111

Joy

[God] will yet fill your mouth with laughter
    and your lips with shouts of joy.

JOB 8:21

"You will go out in joy
    and be led forth in peace;
the mountains and hills
    will burst into song before you,
and all the trees of the field
    will clap their hands," declares the LORD.

ISAIAH 55:12

Jesus said, "Until now you have not
asked for anything in my name. Ask
and you will receive, and your joy will
be complete."

JOHN 16:24

Justice

Speak up for those who cannot speak for themselves,
    for the rights of all who are destitute.
Speak up and judge fairly;
    defend the rights of the poor and needy.

PROVERBS 31:8–9

Learn to do right!
Seek justice,
    encourage the oppressed.
Defend the cause of the fatherless,
    plead the case of the widow.

ISAIAH 1:17

He has shown all you people what is good.
    And what does the LORD require of you?
To act justly and to love mercy
    and to walk humbly with your God.

MICAH 6:8 TNIV

God's judgment is right, and as a result you will be
counted worthy of the kingdom of God.

2 THESSALONIANS 1:5

Justice

The LORD is righteous,
*   he loves justice;*
*   the upright will see his face.*

PSALM 11:7 TNIV

The LORD is known by his justice;
    the wicked are ensnared by the work of their
        hands.

PSALM 9:16

Many seek an audience with a ruler,
    but it is from the LORD that man finds justice.

PROVERBS 29:26

The LORD is a God of justice.
*   Blessed are all who wait for him!*

ISAIAH 30:18

Kindness

Those who are kind to the poor lend to the LORD,
and he will reward them for what they have
done.

PROVERBS 19:17 TNIV

Those who are kind benefit themselves,
but the cruel bring ruin on themselves.

PROVERBS 11:17 TNIV

Be kind and compassionate to one another, forgiving
each other, just as in Christ God forgave you. Be
imitators of God, therefore, as dearly loved children
and live a life of love, just as Christ loved us and
gave himself up for us as a fragrant offering and
sacrifice to God.

EPHESIANS 4:32–5:2

Make every effort to add to your faith goodness;
and to goodness, knowledge; and to knowledge,
self-control; and to self-control perseverance; and to
perseverance, godliness; and to godliness, brotherly
kindness; and to brotherly kindness, love.

2 PETER 1:5–7

Kindness

Make sure that nobody pays back wrong for wrong, but always try to be kind to each other and to everyone else.

1 THESSALONIANS 5:15

As God's chosen people, holy and dearly loved, clothe yourselves with compassion, kindness, humility, gentleness and patience.

COLOSSIANS 3:12

Whoever is kind to the needy honors God.

PROVERBS 14:31

Jesus said, "In everything, do to others what you would have them do to you, for this sums up the Law and the Prophets."

MATTHEW 7:12

When the kindness and love of God our Savior appeared, he saved us, not because of righteous things we had done, but because of his mercy.

TITUS 3:4 – 5

Promises for Women from the NIV

Kingdom of God

"I tell you the truth," Jesus said to them, "No one who has left home or wife or brothers or parents or children for the sake of the kingdom of God will fail to receive many times as much in this age and, in the age to come, eternal life."

LUKE 18:29–30

The LORD has established his throne in heaven,
    and his kingdom rules over all.

PSALM 103:19

[God] has rescued us from the dominion of darkness and brought us into the kingdom of the Son he loves, in whom we have redemption, the forgiveness of sin.

COLOSSIANS 1:13–14

All you have made will praise you, O LORD;
    your saints will extol you.
They will tell of the glory of your kingdom
    and speak of your might,
so that all men may know of your mighty acts
    and the glorious splendor of your kingdom.
Your kingdom is an everlasting kingdom,
    and your dominion endures through all
        generations.

PSALM 145:10–13

Kingdom of God

The kingdom of God is not a matter of eating and drinking, but of righteousness, peace and joy in the Holy Spirit, because anyone who serves Christ in this way is pleasing to God and approved by men.

ROMANS 14:17–18

Since we are receiving a kingdom that cannot be shaken, let us be thankful, and so worship God acceptably with reverence and awe.

HEBREWS 12:28

Jesus said, "Do not be afraid, little flock, for your Father has been pleased to give you the kingdom."

LUKE 12:32

Once, having been asked by the Pharisees when the kingdom of God would come, Jesus replied, "The kingdom of God does not come with your careful observation, nor will people say, 'Here it is,' or 'There it is,' because the kingdom of God is within you."

LUKE 17:20–21

Knowledge

God, who said, "Let light shine out of darkness," made his light shine in our hearts to give us the light of the knowledge of the glory of God in the face of Christ.

2 CORINTHIANS 4:6

Gold there is, and rubies in abundance, but lips that speak knowledge are a rare jewel.

PROVERBS 20:15

Since the day we heard about you, we have not stopped praying for you and asking God to fill you with the knowledge of his will through all spiritual wisdom and understanding.

COLOSSIANS 1:9

Knowledge of the Holy One is understanding.

PROVERBS 9:10

This is my prayer: that your love may abound more and more in knowledge and depth of insight, so that you may be able to discern what is best and may be pure and blameless until the day of Christ.

PHILIPPIANS 1:9–10

Knowledge

Grace and peace be yours in abundance through the knowledge of God and of Jesus our Lord. His divine power has given us everything we need for life and godliness through our knowledge of him who called us by his own glory and goodness.

2 PETER 1:2

The prudent are crowned with knowledge.

PROVERBS 14:18

To the person who pleases him, God gives wisdom, knowledge and happiness.

ECCLESIASTES 2:26 TNIV

Grow in the grace and knowledge of our Lord and Savior Jesus Christ.

2 PETER 3:18

Thanks be to God, who always leads us in triumphal procession in Christ and through us spreads everywhere the fragrance of the knowledge of him.

2 CORINTHIANS 2:14

Life

You have made known to me the paths of life;
   you will fill me with joy in your presence.

ACTS 2:28

With you, [O LORD,] is the fountain of life;
   in your light we see light.

PSALM 36:9

Jesus declared, "I am the bread of life. He who comes
to me will never go hungry, and he who believes in
me will never be thirsty."

JOHN 6:35

If the Spirit of him who raised Jesus from the dead is
living in you, he who raised Christ from the dead
will also give life to your mortal bodies through his
Spirit, who lives in you.

ROMANS 8:11

The fear of the LORD adds length to life.

PROVERBS 10:27

Jesus said, "The Spirit gives life; the flesh counts for
nothing. The words I have spoken to you are spirit
and they are life."

JOHN 6:63

Life

Jesus said, "I have come that they may have life, and have it to the full."

JOHN 10:10

Set your hearts on things above, where Christ is seated at the right hand of God. Set your minds on things above, not on earthly things. For you died, and your life is now hidden with Christ in God. When Christ, who is your life, appears, then you also will appear with him in glory.

COLOSSIANS 3:1–4

Choose life, so that you and your children may live. ... For the LORD is your life, and he will give you many years in the land he swore to give to your fathers, Abraham, Isaac and Jacob.

DEUTERONOMY 30:19–20

Listen, ... accept what I say,
    and the years of your life will be many.

PROVERBS 4:10

Loneliness

Though my father and mother forsake me,
    the LORD will receive me.

PSALM 27:10

A father to the fatherless, a defender of widows,
    is God in his holy dwelling.
God sets the lonely in families.

PSALM 68:5–6

Yet I am always with you;
    you hold me by my right hand.

PSALM 73:23

The LORD watches over the alien
    and sustains the fatherless and the widow.

PSALM 146:9

"I will betroth you to me forever;
    I will betroth you in righteousness and justice,
    in love and compassion.
I will betroth you in faithfulness,
    and you will acknowledge the LORD,"
        declares the LORD.

HOSEA 2:19–20

Loneliness

Jesus said, "I will not leave you as orphans; I will come to you."

JOHN 14:18

The LORD said, "I am with you and will watch over you wherever you go, and I will bring you back to this land. I will not leave you until I have done what I have promised you."

GENESIS 28:15

Come near to God and he will come near to you.

JAMES 4:8

None of us lives to himself alone and none of us dies to himself alone. If we live, we live to the Lord; and if we die, we die to the Lord. So, whether we live or die, we belong to the Lord.

ROMANS 14:7–8

Love

I pray that you, being rooted and established in love, may have power, together with all the saints, to grasp how wide and long and high and deep is the love of Christ, and to know this love that surpasses knowledge—that you may be filled to the measure of all the fullness of God.

EPHESIANS 3:17–19

If you really keep the royal law found in Scripture, "Love your neighbor as yourself," you are doing right.

JAMES 2:8

We love because he first loved us.

1 JOHN 4:19

Dear friends, let us love one another, for love comes from God. Everyone who loves has been born of God and knows God.

1 JOHN 4:7

This is love: not that we loved God, but that he loved us and sent his Son as an atoning sacrifice for our sins.

1 JOHN 4:10

Love

Jesus said, "Love your enemies, do good to them, and lend to them without expecting to get anything back. Then your reward will be great, and you will be sons of the Most High."

LUKE 6:35

Above all, love each other deeply, because love covers over a multitude of sins.

1 PETER 4:8

No one has ever seen God; but if we love one another, God lives in us and his love is made complete in us.

1 JOHN 4:12

Love the LORD your God with all your heart and with all your soul and with all your strength.

DEUTERONOMY 6:5

If anyone acknowledges that Jesus is the Son of God, God lives in him and he in God. And so we know and rely on the love God has for us. God is love. Whoever lives in love lives in God, and God in him.

1 JOHN 4:15–16

Meditation

Do not let this Book of the Law depart from your mouth; meditate on it day and night, so that you may be careful to do everything written in it. Then you will be prosperous and successful.

JOSHUA 1:8

Oh, how I love your law!
    I meditate on it all day long.
Your commands make me wiser than my enemies,
    for they are ever with me.
I have more insight than all my teachers,
    for I meditate on your statutes.

PSALM 119:97–99

May the words of my mouth and the
        meditation of my heart
be pleasing in your sight,
    O LORD, my Rock and my Redeemer.

PSALM 19:14

Let me understand the teaching of your precepts;
    then I will meditate on your wonders.

PSALM 119:27

Meditation

I will meditate on all your works
and consider all your mighty deeds.

PSALM 77:12

Blessed are those
    who do not walk in step with the wicked
or stand in the way that sinners take
    or sit in the company of mockers,
but who delight in the law of the LORD
    and meditate on his law day and night.

PSALM 1:1–2 TNIV

I rise before dawn and cry for help;
    I have put my hope in your word.
My eyes stay open through the watches of the night,
    that I may meditate on your promises.

PSALM 119:147–148

✢

Ministry

Such confidence as this is ours through Christ before God. Not that we are competent in ourselves to claim anything for ourselves, but our competence comes from God. He has made us competent as ministers of a new covenant—not of the letter but of the Spirit; for the letter kills, but the Spirit gives life.

2 CORINTHIANS 3:4–6

Serve wholeheartedly, as if you were serving the Lord, not people, because you know that the Lord will reward each one of you for whatever good you do.

EPHESIANS 6:7–8 TNIV

It was [God] who gave some to be apostles, some to be prophets, some to be evangelists, and some to be pastors and teachers, to prepare God's people for works of service, so that the body of Christ may be built up until we all reach unity in the faith and in the knowledge of the Son of God and become mature, attaining to the whole measure of the fullness of Christ.

EPHESIANS 4:11–13

Ministry

God was reconciling the world to himself in Christ, not counting men's sins against them. And he has committed to us the message of reconciliation. We are therefore Christ's ambassadors, as though God were making his appeal through us.

2 CORINTHIANS 5:19–20

The King will say to those on his right, "Come, you who are blessed by my Father; take your inheritance, the kingdom prepared for you since the creation of the world. For I was hungry and you gave me something to eat, I was thirsty and you gave me something to drink, I was a stranger and you invited me in, I needed clothes and you clothed me, I was sick and you looked after me, I was in prison and you came to visit me." Then the righteous will answer him, "Lord, when did we see you hungry and feed you, or thirsty and give you something to drink? When did we see you a stranger and invite you in, or needing clothes and clothe you? When did we see you sick or in prison and go to visit you?" The King will reply, "I tell you the truth, whatever you did for one of the least of these brothers of mine, you did for me."

MATTHEW 25:34–40

Money

Keep your lives free from the love of money and be content with what you have, because God has said, "Never will I leave you; never will I forsake you."

HEBREWS 13:5

Whoever gathers money little by little makes it grow.

PROVERBS 13:11 TNIV

Remember the LORD your God, for it is he who gives you the ability to produce wealth, and so confirms his covenant, which he swore to your forefathers, as it is today.

DEUTERONOMY 8:18

My God will meet all your needs according to his glorious riches in Christ Jesus.

PHILIPPIANS 4:19

Honor the LORD with your wealth,
     with the firstfruits of all your crops;
then your barns will be filled to overflowing,
     and your vats will brim over with new wine.

PROVERBS 3:9–10

Let no debt remain outstanding, except the continuing debt to love one another, for whoever loves others has fulfilled the law.

ROMANS 13:8 TNIV

Money

"Bring the whole tithe into the storehouse, that there may be food in my house. Test me in this," says the LORD Almighty, "and see if I will not throw open the floodgates of heaven and pour out so much blessing that you will not have room enough for it."

MALACHI 3:10

Those who trust in their riches will fall, but the righteous will thrive like a green leaf.

PROVERBS 11:28 TNIV

Jesus said, "Go, sell everything you have and give to the poor, and you will have treasure in heaven."

MARK 10:21

Jesus said, "Do not store up for yourselves treasures on earth, where moth and rust destroy, and where thieves break in and steal. But store up for yourselves treasures in heaven, where moth and rust do not destroy, and where thieves do not break in and steal. For where your treasure is, there your heart will be also."

MATTHEW 6:19–21

Obedience

It is not those who hear the law who are righteous in God's sight, but it is those who obey the law who will be declared righteous.

ROMANS 2:13

I command you today to love the LORD your God, to walk in his ways, and to keep his commands, decrees and laws; then you will live and increase, and the LORD your God will bless you in the land you are entering to possess.

DEUTERONOMY 30:16

Just as through the disobedience of the one man the many were made sinners, so also through the obedience of the one man the many will be made righteous.

ROMANS 5:19

Jesus said, "Everyone who hears these words of mine and puts them into practice is like a wise man who built his house on the rock. The rain came down, the streams rose, and the winds blew and beat against that house; yet it did not fall, because it had its foundation on the rock."

MATTHEW 7:24–25

Obedience

Jesus replied, "Blessed rather are those who hear the word of God and obey it."

If you fully obey the LORD your God and carefully follow all his commands I give you today, the LORD your God will set you high above all the nations on earth.

DEUTERONOMY 28:1

Jesus said, "If you obey my commands, you will remain in my love, just as I have obeyed my Father's commands and remain in his love. I have told you this so that my joy may be in you and that your joy may be complete."

JOHN 15:10–11

It is the LORD your God you must follow, and him you must revere. Keep his commands and obey him; serve him and hold fast to him.

DEUTERONOMY 13:4

If anyone obeys his word, God's love is truly made complete in him. This is how we know we are in him.

1 JOHN 2:5

Patience

We pray this in order that you may live a life worthy of the Lord and may please him in every way: bearing fruit in every good work, growing in the knowledge of God, being strengthened with all power according to his glorious might so that you may have great endurance and patience.

COLOSSIANS 1:10–11

Be joyful in hope, patient in affliction, faithful in prayer.

ROMANS 12:12

Through patience a ruler can be persuaded,
and a gentle tongue can break a bone.

PROVERBS 25:15

Be patient, then, until the Lord's coming. See how the farmer waits for the land to yield its valuable crop and how patient he is for the autumn and spring rains. You too, be patient and stand firm, because the Lord's coming is near.

JAMES 5:7–8

Patience

If we hope for what we do not yet have, we wait for it patiently.

ROMANS 8:25

Those who are patient have great understanding.

PROVERBS 14:29 TNIV

The end of a matter is better than its beginning, and patience is better than pride.

ECCLESIASTES 7:8

I was shown mercy so that in me, the worst of sinners, Christ Jesus might display his unlimited patience as an example for those who would believe on him and receive eternal life.

1 TIMOTHY 1:16

The Lord is not slow in keeping his promise, as some understand slowness. He is patient with you, not wanting anyone to perish, but everyone to come to repentance.

2 PETER 3:9

Peace

The LORD blesses his people with peace.

PSALM 29:11

Since we have been justified through faith, we have peace with God through our Lord Jesus Christ.

ROMANS 5:1

Aim for perfection, listen to my appeal, be of one mind, live in peace. And the God of love and peace will be with you.

2 CORINTHIANS 13:11

I will listen to what God the LORD will say;
  he promises peace to his people, his saints.

PSALM 85:8

The mind controlled by the sinful nature is death, but the mind controlled by the Spirit is life and peace.

ROMANS 8:6 TNIV

Glory, honor and peace for everyone who does good: first for the Jew, then for the Gentile. For God does not show favoritism.

ROMANS 2:10–11

Peace

Great peace have they that love your law,
  and nothing can make them stumble.

PSALM 119:165

You will keep in perfect peace
  those whose minds are steadfast,
  because they trust in you.

ISAIAH 26:3 TNIV

Peacemakers who sow in peace raise a
harvest of righteousness.

JAMES 3:18

When the LORD takes pleasure in anyone's way,
  he causes their enemies to make peace with them.

PROVERBS 16:7 TNIV

Consider the blameless, observe the upright;
  a future awaits those who seek peace.

PSALM 37:37 TNIV

Peace

Jesus said, "Blessed are the peacemakers, for they will be called children of God."

MATTHEW 5:9 TNIV

Jesus said, "Peace I leave with you; my peace I give you. I do not give to you as the world gives."

JOHN 14:27

[Christ] himself is our peace, who has made the two one and has destroyed the barrier, the dividing wall of hostility.

EPHESIANS 2:14

The kingdom of God is not a matter of eating and drinking, but of righteousness, peace and joy in the Holy Spirit, because anyone who serves Christ in this way is pleasing to God and approved by men. Let us therefore make every effort to do what leads to peace and to mutual edification.

ROMANS 14:17–19

Peace

Let the peace of Christ rule in your hearts, since as members of one body you were called to peace.

COLOSSIANS 3:15

The peace of God, which transcends all understanding, will guard your hearts and your minds in Christ Jesus.

PHILIPPIANS 4:7

Grace and peace be yours in abundance through the knowledge of God and of Jesus our Lord.

2 PETER 1:2

Perseverance

We consider blessed those who have persevered. You have heard of Job's perseverance and have seen what the Lord finally brought about. The Lord is full of compassion and mercy.

JAMES 5:11

Blessed are those who persevere under trial, because when they have stood the test, they will receive the crown of life that God has promised to those who love him.

JAMES 1:12 TNIV

Not that I have already obtained all this, or have already been made perfect, but I press on to take hold of that for which Christ Jesus took hold of me.

PHILIPPIANS 3:12

The God of all grace, who called you to his eternal glory in Christ, after you have suffered a little while, will himself restore you and make you strong, firm and steadfast.

1 PETER 5:10

Let us not become weary in doing good, for at the proper time we will reap a harvest if we do not give up.

GALATIANS 6:9

Perseverance

The testing of your faith develops perseverance. Perseverance must finish its work so that you may be mature and complete, not lacking anything.

JAMES 1:3–4

You need to persevere so that when you have done the will of God, you will receive what he has promised.

HEBREWS 10:36

To those who by persistence in doing good seek glory, honor and immortality, he will give eternal life.

ROMANS 2:7

Watch your life and doctrine closely. Persevere in them, because if you do, you will save both yourself and your hearers.

1 TIMOTHY 4:16

We also rejoice in our sufferings, because we know that suffering produces perseverance; perseverance, character; and character, hope.

ROMANS 5:3–4

Possessions

If I give all I possess to the poor and surrender my body to the flames, but have not love, I gain nothing.

1 CORINTHIANS 13:3

As servants of God we commend ourselves in every way: . . . poor, yet making many rich; having nothing, and yet possessing everything.

2 CORINTHIANS 6:4, 10

Jesus answered, "If you want to be perfect, go, sell your possessions and give to the poor, and you will have treasure in heaven. Then come, follow me."

MATTHEW 19:21

Jesus said, "Do not store up for yourselves treasures on earth, where moth and rust destroy, and where thieves break in and steal. But store up for yourselves treasures in heaven, where moth and rust do not destroy, and where thieves do not break in and steal. For where your treasure is, there your heart will be also."

MATTHEW 6:19–21

Delight yourself in the LORD
    and he will give you the desires of your heart.

PSALM 37:4

Possessions

When God gives people wealth and possessions, and the ability to enjoy them, to accept their lot and be happy in their toil—this is a gift of God.

ECCLESIASTES 5:19 TNIV

Jesus said, "Watch out! Be on your guard against all kinds of greed; life does not consist in an abundance of possessions."

LUKE 12:15 TNIV

You sympathized with those in prison and joyfully accepted the confiscation of your property, because you knew that you yourselves had better and lasting possessions.

HEBREWS 10:34

Jesus said, "Seek first his kingdom and his righteousness, and all these things will be given to you as well."

MATTHEW 6:33

The LORD said,
"Ask of me,
and I will make the nations your inheritance,
the ends of the earth your possession."

PSALM 2:8

Power

His divine power has given us everything we need for life and godliness through our knowledge of him who called us by his own glory and goodness.

2 PETER 1:3

The God of Israel gives power and strength to his people.

PSALM 68:35

By his power God raised the Lord from the dead, and he will raise us also.

1 CORINTHIANS 6:14

The LORD says, "I have raised you up for this very purpose, that I might show you my power and that my name might be proclaimed in all the earth."

EXODUS 9:16

The voice of the LORD is powerful.

PSALM 29:4

Wisdom makes one wise person more powerful than ten rulers in a city.

ECCLESIASTES 7:19 TNIV

Power

He gives strength to the weary
and increases the power of the weak.

ISAIAH 40:29

[The Lord] said to me, "My grace is sufficient for you, for my power is made perfect in weakness." Therefore I will boast all the more gladly about my weaknesses, so that Christ's power may rest on me.

2 CORINTHIANS 12:9

I am the LORD, the God of all mankind. Is anything too hard for me?

JEREMIAH 32:27

God did not give us a spirit of timidity,
but a spirit of power.

2 TIMOTHY 1:7

I am not ashamed of the gospel, because it is the power of God for the salvation of everyone who believes.

ROMANS 1:16

Praise & Worship

Come, let us bow down in worship,
     let us kneel before the LORD our Maker.

Let everything that has breath praise the LORD.

PSALM 150:6

*I urge you, . . . in view of God's mercy,
to offer your bodies as living sacrifices,
holy and pleasing to God—this is your
spiritual act of worship.*

ROMANS 12:1

The trumpeters and singers joined in unison, as with
one voice, to give praise and thanks to the LORD.
Accompanied by trumpets, cymbals and other instruments, they raised their voices in praise to the LORD
and sang:

"He is good;
     his love endures forever."

Then the temple of the LORD was filled with a
cloud, and the priests could not perform their service
because of the cloud, for the glory of the LORD filled
the temple of God.

2 CHRONICLES 5:13–14

Praise & Worship

I will praise you, O Lord my God, with all my heart;
   I will glorify your name forever.
For great is your love toward me;
      you have delivered me from the depths of
         the grave.

PSALM 86:12–13

The heavens praise your wonders, O LORD,
      your faithfulness too, in the assembly of the
         holy ones.

PSALM 89:5

Whenever the living creatures give glory, honor and
thanks to him who sits on the throne and who lives
for ever and ever, the twenty-four elders fall down
before him who sits on the throne, and worship him
who lives for ever and ever. They lay their crowns
before the throne and say:

   "You are worthy, our Lord and God,
         to receive glory and honor and power,
      for you created all things,
         and by your will they were created
         and have their being."

REVELATION 4:9–11

219

Prayer

The LORD is far from the wicked
  but he hears the prayer of the righteous.

PROVERBS 15:29

The prayer offered in faith will make the sick person
well; the Lord will raise him up. If he has sinned, he
will be forgiven.

JAMES 5:15

Let everyone who is godly pray to you
  while you may be found;
surely when the mighty waters rise,
  they will not reach him.

PSALM 32:6

The eyes of the Lord are on the righteous and his
ears are attentive to their prayer.

1 PETER 3:12

"If my people, who are called by my name, will
humble themselves and pray and seek my face and
turn from their wicked ways, then will I hear from
heaven and will forgive their sin and will heal their
land," declares the LORD.

2 CHRONICLES 7:14

Prayer

We have not stopped praying for you and asking God to fill you with the knowledge of his will through all spiritual wisdom and understanding.

COLOSSIANS 1:9

Jesus said, "When you stand praying, if you hold anything against anyone, forgive him, so that your Father in heaven may forgive you your sins."

MARK 11:25

You will call upon me and come and pray to me, and I will listen to you. You will seek me and find me when you seek me with all your heart.

JEREMIAH 29:12–13

The prayer of a righteous person is powerful and effective.

JAMES 5:16 TNIV

Jesus said, "When you pray, go into your room, close the door and pray to your Father, who is unseen. Then your Father, who sees what is done in secret, will reward you."

MATTHEW 6:6

Prayer

Jesus said, "I tell you the truth, my Father will give you whatever you ask in my name. Until now you have not asked for anything in my name. Ask and you will receive, and your joy will be complete."

JOHN 16:23–24

The Spirit helps us in our weakness. We do not know what we ought to pray for, but the Spirit himself intercedes for us with groans that words cannot express.

ROMANS 8:26

I call to God,
    and the LORD saves me.
Evening, morning and noon
    I cry out in distress,
    and he hears my voice.

PSALM 55:16–17

Do not be anxious about anything, but in everything, by prayer and petition, with thanksgiving, present your requests to God. And the peace of God, which transcends all understanding, will guard your hearts and your minds in Christ Jesus.

PHILIPPIANS 4:6–7

Prayer

"Before they call I will answer;
     while they are still speaking I will hear,"
        says the LORD.

ISAIAH 65:24

What other nation is so great as to have their gods near them the way the LORD our God is near us whenever we pray to him?

DEUTERONOMY 4:7

Jesus said, "If you remain in me and my words remain in you, ask whatever you wish, and it will be given you."

JOHN 15:7

Jesus said, "This, then, is how you should pray:
" 'Our Father in heaven,
hallowed be your name,
your kingdom come,
your will be done
     on earth as it is in heaven.
Give us today our daily bread.
Forgive us our debts,
     as we also have forgiven our debtors.
And lead us not into temptation,
but deliver us from the evil one.' "

MATTHEW 6:9-13

Priorities

Look to the LORD and his strength;
    seek his face always.
Remember the wonders he has done,
    his miracles, and the judgments he pronounced.

1 CHRONICLES 16:11–12

O God, you are my God,
    earnestly I seek you;
my soul thirsts for you,
    my body longs for you,
in a dry and weary land
    where there is no water.

PSALM 63:1

Imitate those who through faith and patience inherit
what has been promised.

HEBREWS 6:12

We fix our eyes not on what is seen, but on what is
unseen. For what is seen is temporary, but what is
unseen is eternal.

2 CORINTHIANS 4:18

Priorities

Jesus said, "If anyone would come after me, he must deny himself and take up his cross and follow me. For whoever wants to save his life will lose it, but whoever loses his life for me will find it."

MATTHEW 16:24–25

Jesus said, "Do not worry, saying, 'What shall we eat?' or 'What shall we drink?' or 'What shall we wear?' Seek first [God's] kingdom and his righteousness, and all these things will be given to you as well."

MATTHEW 6:31, 33

He who pursues righteousness and love finds life, prosperity and honor.

PROVERBS 21:21

Let us fix our eyes on Jesus, the author and perfecter of our faith, who for the joy set before him endured the cross, scorning its shame, and sat down at the right hand of the throne of God.

HEBREWS 12:2

Protection

If you make the Most High your dwelling—
     even the LORD, who is my refuge—
then no harm will befall you,
     no disaster will come near your tent.
For he will command his angels concerning you
     to guard you in all your ways.

PSALM 91:9–11

The LORD will keep you from all harm—
     he will watch over your life;
the LORD will watch over your coming and going
     both now and forevermore.

PSALM 121:7–8

"No weapon forged against you will prevail,
     and you will refute every tongue that
          accuses you.
This is the heritage of the servants of the LORD,
     and this is their vindication from me,"
          declares the LORD.

ISAIAH 54:17

The Lord watches over all who love him.

PSALM 145:20

Protection

The Lord is faithful, and he will strengthen and
protect you from the evil one.

2 THESSALONIANS 3:3

The LORD loves the just
   and will not forsake his faithful ones.
They will be protected forever.

PSALM 37:28

"Because he loves me," says the LORD, "I will
            rescue him;
   I will protect him, for he acknowledges my name.
He will call upon me, and I will answer him;
   I will be with him in trouble,
   I will deliver him and honor him."

PSALM 91:14–15

The eternal God is your refuge,
   and underneath are the everlasting arms.

DEUTERONOMY 33:27

Provision

The LORD will guide you always;
> he will satisfy your needs in a sun-scorched land
> and will strengthen your frame.
You will be like a well-watered garden,
> like a spring whose waters never fail.

Jesus said, "Your Father knows what you need before you ask him."

MATTHEW 6:8

How priceless is your unfailing love, O God!
> People take refuge in the shadow of your wings.
They feast on the abundance of your house;
> you give them drink from your river of delights.

PSALM 36:7–8 TNIV

Jesus said, "If that is how God clothes the grass of the field, which is here today and tomorrow is thrown into the fire, will he not much more clothe you, O you of little faith? So do not worry, saying, 'What shall we eat?' or 'What shall we drink?' or 'What shall we wear?' For the pagans run after all these things, and your heavenly Father knows that you need them."

MATTHEW 6:30–32

Provision

My God will meet all your needs according to his glorious riches in Christ Jesus.

PHILIPPIANS 4:19

[God] has shown kindness by giving you rain from heaven and crops in their seasons; he provides you with plenty of food and fills your hearts with joy.

ACTS 14:17

Command those who are rich in this present world not to be arrogant nor to put their hope in wealth, which is so uncertain, but to put their hope in God, who richly provides us with everything for our enjoyment.

1 TIMOTHY 6:17

God is able to make all grace abound to you, so that in all things at all times, having all that you need, you will abound in every good work.

2 CORINTHIANS 9:8

⌘

Purity

How can those who are young keep their way pure?
    By living according to your word.
I have hidden your word in my heart
    that I might not sin against you.

PSALM 119:9, 11 TNIV

One who loves a pure heart and who
speaks with grace
will have the king for a friend.

PROVERBS 22:11 TNIV

The wisdom that comes from above is first of all
pure; then peace-loving, considerate, submissive, full
of mercy and good fruit, impartial and sincere.

JAMES 3:17

If we walk in the light, as he is in the light, we have
fellowship with one another, and the blood of Jesus,
his Son, purifies us from all sin.

1 JOHN 1:7

Don't let anyone look down on you because you are
young, but set an example for the believers in
speech, in life, in love, in faith and in purity.

1 TIMOTHY 4:12

Purity

Come near to God and he will come near to you. Wash your hands, you sinners, and purify your hearts, you double-minded. Grieve, mourn and wail. Change your laughter to mourning and your joy to gloom. Humble yourselves before the Lord, and he will lift you up.

JAMES 4:8–10

To the pure, all things are pure, but to those who are corrupted and do not believe, nothing is pure.

TITUS 1:15

LORD, who may dwell in your sanctuary?
    Who may live on your holy hill?
He whose walk is blameless
    and who does what is righteous,
who speaks the truth from his heart.

PSALM 15:1–2

Jesus said, "Blessed are the pure in heart, for they will see God."

MATTHEW 5:8

Purpose

I cry out to God Most High,
    to God, who fulfills his purpose for me.

We constantly pray for you, that our God may count you worthy of his calling, and that by his power he may fulfill every good purpose of yours and every act prompted by your faith.

2 THESSALONIANS 1:11

*Many are the plans in a human heart,
    but it is the LORD's purpose that
        prevails.*

PROVERBS 19:21 TNIV

Because God wanted to make the unchanging nature of his purpose very clear to the heirs of what was promised, he confirmed it with an oath.

HEBREWS 6:17

Everyone who confesses the name of the Lord must turn away from wickedness. . . . Those who cleanse themselves from the latter will be instruments for noble purposes, made holy, useful to the Master and prepared to do any good work.

2 TIMOTHY 2:19, 21 TNIV

Purpose

The LORD will fulfill his purpose for me;
>   your love, O LORD, endures forever—
>   do not abandon the works of your hands.

PSALM 138:8

We know that in all things God works for the good of those who love him, who have been called according to his purpose.

ROMANS 8:28

We are God's workmanship, created in Christ Jesus to do good works, which God prepared in advance for us to do.

EPHESIANS 2:10

The plans of the LORD stand firm forever,
>   the purposes of his heart through all generations.

PSALM 33:11

The LORD Almighty has sworn,
"Surely, as I have planned, so it will be,
>   and as I have purposed, so it will stand."

ISAIAH 14:24

Quietness & Solitude

Better a dry crust with peace and quiet
    than a house full of feasting, with strife.

PROVERBS 17:1

The LORD is my portion;
    therefore I will wait for him.
The LORD is good to those whose hope is in him,
    to the one who seeks him;
it is good to wait quietly
    for the salvation of the LORD.

LAMENTATIONS 3:24–26

I have stilled and quieted my soul;
    like a weaned child with its mother,
    like a weaned child is my soul within me.

PSALM 131:2

The LORD will fight for you; you need only to be still.

EXODUS 14:14

Make it your ambition to lead a quiet life, to mind your own business and to work with your hands.

1 THESSALONIANS 4:11

Quietness & Solitude

Be still, and know that I am God;
I will be exalted among the nations,
I will be exalted in the earth.

PSALM 46:10

The fruit of righteousness will be peace;
the effect of righteousness will be quietness and
confidence forever.

ISAIAH 32:17

I urge, then, first of all, that requests, prayers,
intercession and thanksgiving be made for
everyone—for kings and all those in authority, that
we may live peaceful and quiet lives in all godliness
and holiness. This is good, and pleases God our
Savior, who wants all men to be saved and to come
to a knowledge of the truth.

1 TIMOTHY 2:1–4

Redemption

*[God] redeemed us in order that the
blessing given to Abraham might come
to the Gentiles through Christ Jesus.*

GALATIANS 3:14

It was not with perishable things such as silver or
gold that you were redeemed from the empty way of
life handed down to you from your forefathers, but
with the precious blood of Christ, a lamb without
blemish or defect.

1 PETER 1:18–21

Put your hope in the LORD,
    for with the LORD is unfailing love
    and with him is full redemption.

PSALM 130:7

Praise the LORD. . . .
He provided redemption for his people;
    he ordained his covenant forever—
    holy and awesome is his name.

PSALM 111:1, 9

All have sinned and fall short of the glory of God,
and are justified freely by his grace through the
redemption that came by Christ Jesus.

ROMANS 3:23–24

Redemption

We ourselves, who have the firstfruits of the Spirit, groan inwardly as we wait eagerly for our adoption as sons, the redemption of our bodies.

ROMANS 8:23–24

In [Christ], we have redemption through his blood, the forgiveness of sins, in accordance with the riches of God's grace that he lavished on us with all wisdom and understanding.

EPHESIANS 1:7–8

[God] has rescued us from the dominion of darkness and brought us into the kingdom of the Son he loves, in whom we have redemption, the forgiveness of sins.

COLOSSIANS 1:13–14

"I have swept away your offenses like a cloud,
    your sins like the morning mist.
Return to me,
    for I have redeemed you," says the LORD.

ISAIAH 44:22

Rejection

The LORD will not reject his people;
he will never forsake his inheritance.

PSALM 94:14

Those who know your name will trust in you,
for you, LORD, have never forsaken those who
seek you.

PSALM 9:10

Do not hide your face from me,
do not turn your servant away in anger;
you have been my helper.
Do not reject me or forsake me,
O God my Savior.
Though my father and mother forsake me,
the LORD will receive me.

PSALM 27:9–10

For the sake of his great name the LORD
will not reject his people, because the
LORD was pleased to make you his own.

1 SAMUEL 12:22

Rejection

Jesus said, "All that the Father gives me will come to me, and whoever comes to me I will never drive away. For I have come down from heaven not to do my will but to do the will of him who sent me. And this is the will of him who sent me, that I shall lose none of all that he has given me, but raise them up at the last day."

JOHN 6:37–39

Jesus said, "He who listens to you listens to me; he who rejects you rejects me; but he who rejects me rejects him who sent me."

LUKE 10:16

Looking at his disciples, [Jesus] said, . . .
"Blessed are you when men hate you,
    when they exclude you and insult you
    and reject your name as evil,
        because of the Son of Man."

LUKE 6:20, 22

Relationships

Jesus said, "A new command I give you: Love one another. As I have loved you, so you must love one another. By this all men will know that you are my disciples, if you love one another."

JOHN 13:34–35

Jesus said, "Here I am! I stand at the door and knock. If anyone hears my voice and opens the door, I will come in and eat with him, and he with me."

REVELATION 3:20

One who has unreliable friends soon comes to ruin, but there is a friend who sticks closer than a brother.

PROVERBS 18:24 TNIV

Be devoted to one another in brotherly love. Honor one another above yourselves.

ROMANS 12:10

Walk with the wise and become wise.

PROVERBS 13:20 TNIV

Jesus said, "I tell you the truth, whatever you did for one of the least of these brothers of mine, you did for me."

MATTHEW 25:40

Relationships

Jesus said, "My command is this:
Love each other as I have loved you.
Greater love has no one than this, that
he lay down his life for his friends."

JOHN 15:12–13

Two are better than one,
    because they have a good return for their labor:
If they fall down,
    they can help each other up.
But pity those who fall
    and have no one to help them up!
Also, if two lie down together, they will keep warm.
    But how can one keep warm alone?
Though one may be overpowered,
    two can defend themselves.
A cord of three strands is not quickly broken.

ECCLESIASTES 4:9–12 TNIV

Carry each other's burdens, and in this way you will
fulfill the law of Christ.

GALATIANS 6:2

Renewal

See, I am doing a new thing!
Now it springs up; do you not
perceive it?
I am making a way in the desert
and streams in the wasteland.

ISAIAH 43:19

You have taken off your old self with its practices
and have put on the new self, which is being
renewed in knowledge in the image of its Creator.

COLOSSIANS 3:9–10

This is what the Sovereign LORD says: . . .
"Behold, I will create
new heavens and a new earth.
The former things will not be remembered,
nor will they come to mind."

ISAIAH 65:13, 17

We eagerly await a Savior from there, the Lord
Jesus Christ, who, by the power that enables him to
bring everything under his control, will transform
our lowly bodies so that they will be like his
glorious body.

PHILIPPIANS 3:20–21

Renewal

Be made new in the attitude of your minds.

EPHESIANS 4:23

The LORD says, "I will give you a new heart and put a new spirit in you; I will remove from you your heart of stone and give you a heart of flesh. And I will put my Spirit in you and move you to follow my decrees and be careful to keep my laws."

EZEKIEL 36:26–27

Don't you know that all of us who were baptized into Christ Jesus were baptized into his death? We were therefore buried with him through baptism into death in order that, just as Christ was raised from the dead through the glory of the Father, we too may live a new life.

ROMANS 6:3–4

Create in me a pure heart, O God,
and renew a steadfast spirit
within me.

PSALM 51:10

Though outwardly we are wasting away, yet inwardly we are being renewed day by day.

2 CORINTHIANS 4:16

Repentance

Peter replied, "Repent and be baptized, every one of you, in the name of Jesus Christ for the forgiveness of your sins. And you will receive the gift of the Holy Spirit."

ACTS 2:38

If my people, who are called by my name, will humble themselves and pray and seek my face and turn from their wicked ways, then will I hear from heaven and will forgive their sin and will heal their land.

2 CHRONICLES 7:14

This is what the Sovereign LORD, the Holy One of Israel, says:

"In repentance and rest is your salvation,
in quietness and trust is your strength."

ISAIAH 30:15

Let the wicked forsake their ways
and the unrighteous their thoughts.
Let them turn to the LORD, and he will have mercy
on them,
and to our God, for he will freely pardon.

ISAIAH 55:7 TNIV

Repentance

Jesus said, "I tell you that in the same way there will be more rejoicing in heaven over one sinner who repents than over ninety-nine righteous persons who do not need to repent."

LUKE 15:7

Repent, then, and turn to God, so that your sins may be wiped out, that times of refreshing may come from the Lord.

ACTS 3:19

The Lord is not slow in keeping his promise, as some understand slowness. He is patient with you, not wanting anyone to perish, but everyone to come to repentance.

2 PETER 3:9

Godly sorrow brings repentance that leads to salvation and leaves no regret.

2 CORINTHIANS 7:10

Jesus answered them, "It is not the healthy who need a doctor, but the sick. I have not come to call the righteous, but sinners to repentance."

LUKE 5:31–32

Repentance

Those who conceal their sins do not prosper,
but those who confess and renounce them
find mercy.

PROVERBS 28:13 TNIV

*This is what the LORD says:
"If you repent, I will restore you
that you may serve me."*

JEREMIAH 15:19

"The Redeemer will come to Zion,
to those in Jacob who repent of their sins,"
declares the LORD.

ISAIAH 59:20

Jesus said, "In the same way, I tell you, there is
rejoicing in the presence of the angels of God over
one sinner who repents."

LUKE 15:10

If the wicked turn away from all the sins they have
committed and keep all my decrees and do what is
just and right, they will surely live; they will not die.

EZEKIEL 18:21 TNIV

Repentance

These are the words of the Amen, the faithful and true witness, the ruler of God's creation. "Those whom I love I rebuke and discipline. So be earnest, and repent."

REVELATION 3:14, 19

Jesus said, "If your brother sins, rebuke him, and if he repents, forgive him. If he sins against you seven times in a day, and seven times comes back to you and says, 'I repent,' forgive him."

LUKE 17:3–4

Whenever anyone turns to the Lord, the veil is taken away. Now the Lord is the Spirit, and where the Spirit of the Lord is, there is freedom.

2 CORINTHIANS 3:16–17

Rest

Jesus said, "Come to me, all you who are weary and burdened, and I will give you rest. Take my yoke upon you and learn from me, for I am gentle and humble in heart, and you will find rest for your souls. For my yoke is easy and my burden is light."

MATTHEW 11:28–30

There remains, then, a Sabbath-rest for the people of God; for anyone who enters God's rest also rests from his own work, just as God did from his. Let us, therefore, make every effort to enter that rest.

HEBREWS 4:9–11

This is what the LORD Almighty says, "I will refresh the weary and satisfy the faint."

JEREMIAH 31:25

My soul finds rest in God alone;
my salvation comes from him.
He alone is my rock and my salvation;
he is my fortress, I will never be shaken.

PSALM 62:1–2

Rest

Be at rest once more, O my soul,
for the LORD has been good to you.

PSALM 116:7

Whoever dwells in the shelter of the Most High
will rest in the shadow of the Almighty.

PSALM 91:1 TNIV

My people will live in peaceful dwelling places,
in secure homes,
in undisturbed places of rest.

ISAIAH 32:18

The LORD is my shepherd, I shall not be in want.
He makes me lie down in green pastures,
he leads me beside quiet waters,
he restores my soul.
He guides me in paths of righteousness
for his name's sake.

PSALM 23:1–3

Restoration

The LORD says, "I will search for the lost and bring back the strays. I will bind up the injured and strengthen the weak."

EZEKIEL 34:16

When you and your children return to the LORD your God and obey him with all your heart and with all your soul according to everything I command you today, then the LORD your God will restore your fortunes and have compassion on you.

DEUTERONOMY 30:2–3

"I will restore you to health
    and heal your wounds," declares the LORD.

JEREMIAH 30:17

Though you have made me see troubles, many
        and bitter,
    you will restore my life again;
from the depths of the earth
    you will again bring me up.
You will increase my honor
    and comfort me once again.

PSALM 71:20–21

Restoration

The LORD says,
"You will have plenty to eat, until you are full,
    and you will praise the name of the LORD your
        God,
    who has worked wonders for you;
never again will my people be shamed."

JOEL 2:26

Restore us, O God;
    make your face shine upon us,
    that we may be saved.

PSALM 80:3

The God of all grace, who called you to his eternal
glory in Christ, after you have suffered a little while,
will himself restore you and make you strong, firm
and steadfast.

1 PETER 5:10

Reward

Behold, I am coming soon! My reward is with me, and I will give to everyone according to what he has done.

REVELATION 22:12

Jesus said, "Love your enemies, do good to them, and lend to them without expecting to get anything back. Then your reward will be great, and you will be sons of the Most High."

LUKE 6:35

Jesus said, "Blessed are you when people insult you, persecute you and falsely say all kinds of evil against you because of me. Rejoice and be glad, because great is your reward in heaven."

MATTHEW 5:11–12

I the LORD search the heart
 and examine the mind,
to reward everyone according to their conduct,
 according to what their deeds deserve.

JEREMIAH 17:10 TNIV

Fire will test the quality of each person's work. If what has been built survives, the builder will receive a reward.

1 CORINTHIANS 3:13–14 TNIV

Reward

Whatever you do, work at it with all your heart, as working for the Lord, not for human masters, since you know that you will receive an inheritance from the Lord as a reward. It is the Lord Christ you are serving.

COLOSSIANS 3:23–24 TNIV

Jesus said, "When you pray, go into your room, close the door and pray to your Father, who is unseen. Then your Father, who sees what is done in secret, will reward you."

MATTHEW 6:6

You know that the Lord will reward everyone for whatever good he does.

EPHESIANS 6:8

Jesus said, "If anyone gives even a cup of cold water to one of these little ones who is known to be my disciple, truly I tell you, that person will certainly be rewarded."

MATTHEW 10:42 TNIV

Righteousness

*God made him who had no sin to be sin
for us, so that in him we might become
the righteousness of God.*

2 CORINTHIANS 5:21

Do not let anyone lead you astray. He who does
what is right is righteous, just as [God] is righteous.

1 JOHN 3:7

The eyes of the Lord are on the righteous
and his ears are attentive to their prayer.

1 PETER 3:12

*The fruit of the righteous is a tree of life,
and he who wins souls is wise.*

PROVERBS 11:30

The mouths of the righteous utter wisdom,
and their tongues speak what is just.
The law of their God is in their hearts;
their feet do not slip.

PSALM 37:30–31 TNIV

Righteousness

The path of the righteous is like the first gleam
>   of dawn,
>   shining ever brighter till the full light of day.

PROVERBS 4:18

Jesus said, "Blessed are those who hunger and thirst
for righteousness, for they will be filled."

MATTHEW 5:6

[God] does not take his eyes off the righteous;
>   he enthrones them with kings
>   and exalts them forever.

JOB 36:7

The righteous are as bold as a lion.

PROVERBS 28:1

*In the way of righteousness there is life;
along that path is immortality.*

PROVERBS 12:28

Sacrifice

O Lord, open my lips,
  and my mouth will declare your praise.
The sacrifices of God are a broken spirit;
  a broken and contrite heart,
  O God, you will not despise.

PSALM 51:15, 17

I urge you, . . . in view of God's mercy, to offer your bodies as living sacrifices, holy and pleasing to God—this is your spiritual act of worship.

ROMANS 12:1

Be silent before the Sovereign LORD,
  for the day of the LORD is near.
The LORD has prepared a sacrifice;
  he has consecrated those he has invited.

ZEPHANIAH 1:7

Through Jesus . . . let us continually offer to God a sacrifice of praise—the fruit of lips that confess his name. And do not forget to do good and to share with others, for with such sacrifices God is pleased.

HEBREWS 13:15–16

Sacrifice

I will sacrifice a freewill offering to you;
    I will praise your name, O LORD,
    for it is good.
For he has delivered me from all my troubles,
    and my eyes have looked in triumph on my foes.

PSALM 54:6 – 7

As you come to him, the living Stone—rejected my men but chosen by God and precious to him—you also, like living stones, are being built into a spiritual house to be a holy priesthood, offering spiritual sacrifices acceptable to God through Jesus Christ.

1 PETER 2:4–5

To do what is right and just
    is more acceptable to the LORD
      than sacrifice.

PROVERBS 21:3

Salvation

If you confess with your mouth, "Jesus is Lord," and believe in your heart that God raised him from the dead, you will be saved. For it is with your heart that you believe and are justified, and it is with your mouth that you confess and are saved.

ROMANS 10:9–10

The hour has come for you to wake up from your slumber, because our salvation is nearer now than when we first believed. The night is nearly over; the day is almost here. So let us put aside the deeds of darkness and put on the armor of light.

ROMANS 13:11–12

Like newborn babies, crave pure spiritual milk, so that by it you may grow up in your salvation, now that you have tasted that the Lord is good.

1 PETER 2:2–3

Believe in the Lord Jesus, and you will be saved—you and your household.

ACTS 16:31

Continue to work out your salvation with fear and trembling, for it is God who works in you to will and to act according to his good purpose.

PHILIPPIANS 2:12–13

Salvation

Once made perfect, [Jesus] became the source of eternal salvation for all who obey him.

HEBREWS 5:9

Now is the time of God's favor, now is the day of salvation.

2 CORINTHIANS 6:2

Christ was sacrificed once to take away the sins of many people; and he will appear a second time, not to bear sin, but to bring salvation to those who are waiting for him.

HEBREWS 9:28

The salvation of the righteous comes from the
        LORD;
  he is their stronghold in time of trouble.

PSALM 37:39

God did not appoint us to suffer wrath but to receive salvation through our Lord Jesus Christ. He died for us so that, whether we are awake or asleep, we may live together with him.

1 THESSALONIANS 5:9–10

Satisfaction

My soul will be satisfied as with the richest of foods;
with singing lips my mouth will praise you.

PSALM 63:5

"Come all you who are thirsty,
come to the waters;
and you who have no money,
come, buy and eat!
Come, buy wine and milk
without money and without cost.
Why spend money on what is not bread,
and your labor on what does not satisfy?
Listen, listen to me, and eat what is good,
and your soul will delight in the richest of fare,"
declares the LORD.

ISAIAH 55:1–2

[The LORD] satisfies your desires with good things
so that your youth is renewed like the eagle's.

PSALM 103:5

*You open your hand
and satisfy the desires of every
living thing.*

PSALM 145:16

Satisfaction

The LORD will guide you always;
>he will satisfy your needs in a sun-scorched land
>and will strengthen your frame.
You will be like a well-watered garden,
>like a spring whose waters never fail.

ISAIAH 58:11

*With long life will I satisfy them
and show them my salvation.*

PSALM 91:16 TNIV

People can do nothing better than to eat and drink
and find satisfaction in their toil. This too, I see, is
from the hand of God,

ECCLESIASTES 2:24 TNIV

Jesus said, "Blessed are you who hunger now, for you
will be satisfied."

LUKE 6:21

⌘

Security

Let the beloved of the LORD rest secure in him,
   for he shields him all day long,
   and the one the LORD loves rests between his
      shoulders.

DEUTERONOMY 33:12

The name of the LORD is a strong tower;
   the righteous run to it and are safe.

PROVERBS 18:10

I have set the LORD always before me.
   Because he is at my right hand,
   I will not be shaken.
Therefore my heart is glad and my tongue rejoices;
   my body also will rest secure.

PSALM 16:8–9

Surely the righteous will never be shaken;
   they will be remembered forever.
They will have no fear of bad news;
   their hearts are steadfast, trusting in the LORD.
Their hearts are secure, they will have no fear.

PSALM 112:6–8 TNIV

Security

My people will live in peaceful dwelling places,
  in secure homes,
  in undisturbed places of rest.
Though hail flattens the forest
  and the city is leveled completely,
how blessed you will be.

ISAIAH 32:18–20

Do not take advantage of each other, but fear your
God. I am the LORD your God. Follow my decrees
and be careful to obey my laws, and you will live
safely in the land. Then the land will yield its fruit,
and you will eat your fill and live there in safety.

LEVITICUS 25:17–19

Those who fear the LORD have a secure fortress.

PROVERBS 14:26 TNIV

I will lie down and sleep in peace,
  for you alone, O LORD,
  make me dwell in safety.

PSALM 4:8

Seeking God

[Jesus] says to you, "Ask and it will be given to you; seek and you will find; knock and the door will be opened to you. For everyone who asks receives; he who seeks finds; and to him who knocks, the door will be opened."

LUKE 11:9–10

"You will call upon me and come and pray to me, and I will listen to you. You will seek me and find me when you seek me with all your heart. I will be found by you," declares the LORD.

JEREMIAH 29:12–14

Sow for yourselves righteousness,
    reap the fruit of unfailing love,
and break up your unplowed ground;
    for it is time to seek the LORD,
until he comes
    and showers righteousness on you.

HOSEA 10:12

Let the hearts of those who seek the LORD rejoice.
Look to the LORD and his strength;
    seek his face always.

PSALM 105:3–4

Seeking God

Seek the LORD while he may be found;
   call on him while he is near.
Let the wicked forsake their ways
   and the unrighteous their thoughts.
Let them turn to the LORD and he will have mercy
         on them,
   and to our God, for he will freely pardon.

ISAIAH 55:6–7 TNIV

*Without faith it is impossible to please
God, because anyone who comes to him
must believe that he exists and that he
rewards those who earnestly seek him.*

HEBREWS 11:6

If you will look to God
   and plead with the Almighty,
if you are pure and upright,
   even now he will rouse himself on your behalf
   and restore you to your rightful place.

JOB 8:5–6

Self-Control

Be self-controlled and alert. Your enemy the devil prowls around like a roaring lion looking for someone to devour. Resist him, standing firm in the faith.

1 PETER 5:8–9

No temptation has seized you except what is common to man. And God is faithful; he will not let you be tempted beyond what you can bear. But when you are tempted, he will also provide a way out so that you can stand up under it.

1 CORINTHIANS 10:13

If by the Spirit you put to death the misdeeds of the body, you will live, because those who are led by the Spirit of God are sons of God.

ROMANS 8:13–14

The fruit of the Spirit is . . . self-control.

GALATIANS 5:22–23

Be careful, and watch yourselves closely so that you do not forget the things your eyes have seen or let them slip from your heart as long as you live. Teach them to your children and to their children after them.

DEUTERONOMY 4:9

Self-Control

Live self-controlled, upright and godly lives in this present age, while we wait for the blessed hope— the glorious appearing of our great God and Savior, Jesus Christ.

TITUS 2:12–13

The end of all things is near. Therefore be clear minded and self-controlled so that you can pray.

1 PETER 4:7

Since we belong to the day, let us be self-controlled, putting on faith and love as a breastplate, and the hope of salvation as a helmet.

1 THESSALONIANS 5:8

Prepare your minds for action; be self-controlled; set your hope fully on the grace to be given you when Jesus Christ is revealed.

1 PETER 1:13

Since an overseer is entrusted with God's work, he must be blameless—not overbearing, not quick-tempered, not given to drunkenness, not violent. . . . Rather he must be . . . self-controlled, upright, holy and disciplined.

TITUS 1:7–8

Self-Esteem

The LORD says,
"You are precious and honored in
my sight,
and . . . I love you."

ISAIAH 43:4

Do you not know that your body is a temple of the
Holy Spirit, who is in you, whom you have received
from God? You are not your own; you were bought at
a price. Therefore honor God with your body.

1 CORINTHIANS 6:19–20

For you created my inmost being;
    you knit me together in my mother's womb.
I praise you because I am fearfully and wonderfully
        made;
    your works are wonderful,
    I know that full well.

PSALM 139:13–14

Jesus said, "Are not two sparrows sold for a penny?
Yet not one of them will fall to the ground apart
from the will of your Father: And even the very hairs
of your head are all numbered. So don't be afraid;
you are worth more than many sparrows."

MATTHEW 10:29–30

Self-Esteem

[God] chose us in him before the creation of the world to be holy and blameless in his sight. In love he predestined us to be adopted as his sons through Jesus Christ, in accordance with his pleasure and will.

EPHESIANS 1:4–5

"I have engraved you on the palms of my hands," declares the LORD.

ISAIAH 49:16

Know that the LORD is God.
 It is he who made us, and we are his;
 we are his people, the sheep of his pasture.

PSALM 100:3

[You] have put on the new self, which is being renewed in knowledge in the image of its Creator.

COLOSSIANS 3:10

Don't you know that you yourselves are God's temple and that God's Spirit lives in you?

1 CORINTHIANS 3:16

Service

Though I am free and belong to no man, I make myself a slave to everyone, to win as many as possible.... I have become all things to all men so that by all possible means I might save some.

1 CORINTHIANS 9:19, 22

It was [Christ] who gave some to be apostles, some to be prophets, some to be evangelists, and some to be pastors and teachers, to prepare God's people for works of service, so that the body of Christ may be built up until we all reach unity in the faith and in the knowledge of the Son of God and become mature, attaining to the whole measure of the fullness of Christ.

EPHESIANS 4:11–13

Jesus said, "Whoever serves me must follow me; and where I am, my servant also will be. My Father will honor the one who serves me."

JOHN 12:26

Serve wholeheartedly, as if you were serving the Lord, not people, because you know that the Lord will reward each one of you for whatever good you do.

EPHESIANS 6:7–8 TNIV

Service

There are different kinds of service, but the same Lord.

1 CORINTHIANS 12:5

Each one should use whatever gift he has received to serve others, faithfully administering God's grace in its various forms. If anyone speaks, he should do it as one speaking the very words of God. If anyone serves, he should do it with the strength God provides, so that in all things God may be praised through Jesus Christ.

1 PETER 4:10–11

Whatever you do, work at it with all your heart, as working for the Lord, not for human masters, since you know that you will receive an inheritance from the Lord as a reward. It is the Lord Christ you are serving.

COLOSSIANS 3:23–24 TNIV

Acknowledge the God of your father, and serve him with wholehearted devotion and with a willing mind, for the LORD searches every heart and understands every motive behind the thoughts.

1 CHRONICLES 28:9

Sincerity

Love must be sincere. Hate what is evil; cling to what is good. Be devoted to one another in brotherly love. Honor one another above yourselves.

ROMANS 12:9–10

For Christ, our Passover lamb, has been sacrificed. Therefore let us keep the Festival, not with the old yeast, the yeast of malice and wickedness, but with bread without yeast, the bread of sincerity and truth.

1 CORINTHIANS 5:7–8

Now this is our boast: Our conscience testifies that we have conducted ourselves in the world, and especially in our relations with you, in the holiness and sincerity that are from God. We have done so not according to worldly wisdom but according to God's grace.

2 CORINTHIANS 1:12

The goal of this command is love, which comes from a pure heart and a good conscience and sincere faith.

1 TIMOTHY 1:5

Sincerity

Since we have a great priest over the house of God, let us draw near to God with a sincere heart in full assurance of faith, having our hearts sprinkled to cleanse us from a guilty conscience and having our bodies washed with pure water. Let us hold unswervingly to the hope we profess, for he who promised is faithful.

HEBREWS 10:21–23

My words come from an upright heart;
my lips sincerely speak what I know.

JOB 33:3

Unlike so many, we do not peddle the word of God for profit. On the contrary, in Christ we speak before God with sincerity, as those sent from God.

2 CORINTHIANS 2:17 TNIV

Now that you have purified yourselves by obeying the truth so that you have sincere love for each other, love one another deeply, from the heart.

1 PETER 1:22 TNIV

Speech

Let your conversation be always full of grace, seasoned with salt, so that you may know how to answer everyone.

COLOSSIANS 4:6

In your teaching show integrity, seriousness and soundness of speech that cannot be condemned, so that those who oppose you may be ashamed because they have nothing bad to say about us.

TITUS 2:7–8

Moses said to the LORD, "O Lord, I have never been eloquent, neither in the past nor since you have spoken to your servant. I am slow of speech and tongue." The LORD said to him, "Who gave man his mouth? Who makes him deaf or mute? Who gives him sight or makes him blind? Is it not I, the LORD? Now go; I will help you speak and will teach you what to say."

EXODUS 4:10–12

Jesus said, "Do not worry beforehand about what to say. Just say whatever is given you at the time, for it is not you speaking, but the Holy Spirit."

MARK 13:11

Speech

Whoever would love life and see good days must keep his tongue from evil and his lips from deceitful speech.

1 PETER 3:10

One who loves a pure heart and who speaks
                with grace
        will have the king for a friend.

PROVERBS 22:11 TNIV

Pleasant words are a honeycomb,
        sweet to the soul and healing to the bones.

PROVERBS 16:24

The speech of the upright rescues them.

PROVERBS 12:6

The quiet words of the wise are more to be heeded
        than the shouts of a ruler of fools.

ECCLESIASTES 9:17

Those who guard their mouths and their tongues
        keep themselves from calamity.

PROVERBS 21:23 TNIV

Spiritual Growth

Those who belong to Christ Jesus have crucified the sinful nature with its passions and desires. Since we live by the Spirit, let us keep in step with the Spirit.

GALATIANS 5:24–25

Put on the full armor of God, so that when the day of evil comes, you may be able to stand your ground, and after you have done everything, to stand. Stand firm then, with the belt of truth buckled around your waist, with the breastplate of righteousness in place, and with your feet fitted with the readiness that comes from the gospel of peace. In addition to all this, take up the shield of faith, with which you can extinguish all the flaming arrows of the evil one. Take the helmet of salvation and the sword of the Spirit, which is the word of God.

EPHESIANS 6:13–18

Jesus said, "Whoever lives by the truth comes into the light, so that it may be seen plainly that what he has done has been done through God."

JOHN 3:21

Jesus said, "I am the vine; you are the branches. If you remain in me and I in you, you will bear much fruit; apart from me you can do nothing."

JOHN 15:5 TNIV

Spiritual Growth

Like newborn babies, crave pure spiritual milk, so
that by it you may grow up in your salvation, now
that you have tasted that the Lord is good.

*Do your best to present yourself to God
as one approved, a workman who does
not need to be ashamed and who
correctly handles the word of truth.*

2 TIMOTHY 2:15

We will no longer be infants, tossed back and forth
by the waves, and blown here and there by every
wind of teaching and by the cunning and craftiness
of men in their deceitful scheming. Instead, speaking
the truth in love, we will in all things grow up into
him who is the Head, that is, Christ.

EPHESIANS 4:14–15

Keep your father's commands
    and do not forsake your mother's teaching.
For these commands are a lamp,
    this teaching is a light,
and the corrections of discipline
    are the way to life.

PROVERBS 6:20, 23

Stability

I have set the LORD always before me.
Because he is at my right hand,
I will not be shaken.

PSALM 16:8

You, O LORD, have delivered my soul from death,
my eyes from tears,
my feet from stumbling,
that I may walk before the LORD
in the and of the living.

PSALM 116:8–9

My soul finds rest in God alone;
my salvation comes from him.
He alone is my rock and my salvation;
he is my fortress, I will never be shaken.

PSALM 62:1–2

The God of all grace, who called you to his eternal
glory in Christ, after you have suffered a little while,
will himself restore you and make you strong, firm
and steadfast.

1 PETER 5:10

Stability

The LORD makes firm the steps
   of those who delight in him;
though they stumble, they will not fall,
   for the LORD upholds them with his hand.

PSALM 37:23–24 TNIV

Whoever loves his brother lives in the light, and
there is nothing in him to make him stumble.

1 JOHN 2:10

Great peace have they that love your law,
   and nothing can make them stumble.

PSALM 119:165

To him who is able to keep you from falling and to
present you before his glorious presence without
fault and with great joy—to the only God our Savior
be glory, majesty, power and authority, through
Jesus Christ our Lord, before all ages, now and
forevermore! Amen.

JUDE 1:24–25

Stewardship

Each one should use whatever gift he has received to serve others, faithfully administering God's grace in its various forms. If anyone speaks, he should do it as one speaking the very words of God. If anyone serves, he should do it with the strength God provides, so that in all things God may be praised through Jesus Christ.

1 PETER 4:10–11

Jesus said, "The kingdom of heaven will be like ... a man going on a journey, who called his servants and entrusted his property to them. To one he gave five talents of money, to another two talents, and to another one talent, each according to his ability. Then he went on his journey. The man who had received the five talents went at once and put his money to work and gained five more.... After a long time the master of those servants returned and settled accounts with them. The man who had received the five talents brought the other five. 'Master,' he said, 'you entrusted me with five talents. See, I have gained five more.' His master replied, 'Well done, good and faithful servant! You have been faithful with a few things; I will put you in charge of many things. Come and share your master's happiness!'"

MATTHEW 25:1, 14–16, 19–21

Stewardship

The Lord answered, "Who then is the faithful and wise manager, whom the master puts in charge of his servants to give them their food allowance at the proper time? It will be good for that servant whom the master finds doing so when he returns."

LUKE 12:42–43

This, then, is how you ought to regard us: as servants of Christ and as those entrusted with the mysteries God has revealed. Now it is required that those who have been given a trust must prove faithful.

1 CORINTHIANS 4:1–2 TNIV

Jesus said, "From everyone who has been given much, much will be demanded; and from the one who has been entrusted with much, much more will be asked."

LUKE 12:48

Good will come to him who is generous
and lends freely,
who conduct his affairs with justice.

PSALM 112:5

Strength

May he strengthen your hearts so that you will be
blameless and holy in the presence of our God and
Father when our Lord Jesus comes with all his
holy ones.

1 THESSALONIANS 3:13

You do not lack any spiritual gift as you eagerly wait
for our Lord Jesus Christ to be revealed. He will keep
you strong to the end.

1 CORINTHIANS 1:7–8

*God is our refuge and strength,
    an ever-present help in trouble.*

PSALM 46:1

Those who hope in the LORD
    will renew their strength.
They will soar on wings like eagles;
    they will run and not grow weary,
    they will walk and not be faint.

ISAIAH 40:31

The LORD gives strength to his people.

PSALM 29:11

Strength

I can do everything through [Christ] who gives me strength.

PHILIPPIANS 4:13

"So do not fear, for I am with you;
    do not be dismayed, for I am your God.
I will strengthen you and help you;
    I will uphold you with my righteous right hand,"
      declares the LORD.

ISAIAH 41:10

My flesh and my heart may fail,
    but God is the strength of my heart
    and my portion forever.

PSALM 73:26

O my Strength, I watch for you;
    you, O God, are my fortress, my loving God.
God will go before me
    and will let me gloat over those who slander me.

PSALM 59:9–10

Strength

The LORD is my strength and my shield;
   my heart trusts in him, and I am helped.

PSALM 28:7

The LORD is the strength of his people,
   a fortress of salvation for his
      anointed one.

PSALM 28:8

Blessed are those whose strength is in you,
   who have set their hearts on pilgrimage.
As they pass through the Valley of Baca,
   they make it a place of springs;
   the autumn rains also cover it with pools.
They go from strength to strength,
   till each appears before God in Zion.

PSALM 84:5–7

It is God who arms me with strength
   and makes my way perfect.

PSALM 18:32

Strength

It is God who arms me with strength
and makes my way perfect.
He makes my feet like the feet of a deer;
he enables me to stand on the heights.

2 SAMUEL 22:33–34

The LORD is my strength and my song;
he has become my salvation.
He is my God, and I will praise him,
my father's God, and I will exalt him.

EXODUS 15:2

I will sing of your strength,
in the morning I will sing of your love;
for you are my fortress,
my refuge in times of trouble.

PSALM 59:16

Stress

"I will refresh the weary and satisfy the faint," says the LORD Almighty.

JEREMIAH 31:25

Do not be anxious about anything, but in everything, by prayer and petition, with thanksgiving, present your requests to God. And the peace of God, which transcends all understanding, will guard your hearts and your minds in Christ Jesus.

PHILIPPIANS 4:6–7

May the Lord of peace himself give you peace at all times and in every way. The Lord be with all of you.

2 THESSALONIANS 3:16

Cast your cares on the LORD
and he will sustain you;
he will never let the righteous fall.

PSALM 55:22

The LORD will be your confidence
and will keep your foot from being snared.

PROVERBS 3:26

Stress

You will keep in perfect peace
  those whose minds are steadfast,
  because they trust in you.
Trust in the LORD forever,
  for the LORD, the LORD, is the Rock eternal.

ISAIAH 26:3–4 TNIV

Cast all your anxiety on him because he cares for you.

1 PETER 5:7

Jesus said, "Come to me, all you who are weary and burdened, and I will give you rest. Take my yoke upon you and learn from me, for I am gentle and humble in heart, and you will find rest for your souls. For my yoke is easy and my burden is light."

MATTHEW 11:28–30

This is what the Sovereign LORD, the Holy One of Israel, says:

"In repentance and rest is your salvation,
  in quietness and trust is your strength."

ISAIAH 30:15

Success

Do not let this Book of the Law depart from your mouth; meditate on it day and night, so that you may be careful to do everything written in it. Then you will be prosperous and successful. Have I not commanded you? Be strong and courageous. Do not be terrified; do not be discouraged, for the LORD your God will be with you wherever you go.

JOSHUA 1:8–9

Have faith in the LORD your God and you will be upheld; have faith in his prophets and you will be successful.

2 CHRONICLES 20:20

Blessed are those who fear the LORD,
    who find great delight in his commands.
Their children will be mighty in the land;
    the generation of the upright will be blessed.
Wealth and riches are in their houses,
    and their righteousness endures forever.

PSALM 112:1–3 TNIV

Success

May [God] give you the desire of your heart
    and make all your plans succeed.
We will shout for joy when you are victorious
    and will lift up our banners in the name of
        our God.
May the LORD grant all your requests.

PSALM 20:4

You will have success if you are careful to observe
the decrees and laws that the LORD gave Moses for
Israel. Be strong and courageous. Do not be afraid
or discouraged.

1 CHRONICLES 22:13

Commit to the LORD whatever you do,
   and your plans will succeed.

PROVERBS 16:3

Plans fail for lack of counsel,
    but with many advisers they succeed.

PROVERBS 15:22

Thankfulness

Give thanks in all circumstances, for this is God's will for you in Christ Jesus.

1 THESSALONIANS 5:18

Since we are receiving a kingdom that cannot be shaken, let us be thankful, and so worship God acceptably with reverence and awe.

HEBREWS 12:28

Thanks be to God for his indescribable gift!

2 CORINTHIANS 9:15

Let the word of Christ dwell in you richly as you teach and admonish one another with all wisdom, and as you sing psalms, hymns and spiritual songs with gratitude in your hearts to God.

COLOSSIANS 3:16

The LORD is my strength and my shield;
my heart trusts in him, and I am helped.
My heart leaps for joy
and I will give thanks to him in song.

PSALM 28:7

Thankfulness

Let them give thanks to the LORD for his
      unfailing love
   and his wonderful deeds for humankind,
for he satisfies the thirsty
      and fills the hungry with good things.

PSALM 107:8–9 TNIV

In everything, by prayer and petition, with
thanksgiving, present your requests to God. And the
peace of God, which transcends all understanding,
will guard your hearts and your minds in Christ Jesus.

PHILIPPIANS 4:6–7

Just as you received Christ Jesus as Lord, continue
to live in him, rooted and built up in him,
strengthened in the faith as you were taught, and
overflowing with thankfulness.

COLOSSIANS 2:6–7

*Thanks be to God! He gives us the
victory through our Lord Jesus Christ.*

1 CORINTHIANS 15:57

Thoughts

I the LORD search the heart
    and examine the mind,
to reward everyone according to their conduct,
    according to what their deeds deserve.

JEREMIAH 17:10 TNIV

We demolish arguments and every pretension
that sets itself up against the knowledge of God,
and we take captive every thought to make it
obedient to Christ.

2 CORINTHIANS 10:5

The LORD knows the thoughts of man.

PSALM 94:11

Holy brothers and sisters, who share in the heavenly
calling, fix your thoughts on Jesus, whom we
acknowledge as our apostle and high priest.

HEBREWS 3:1 TNIV

"My thoughts are not your thoughts,
    neither are your ways my ways,"
        declares the LORD.

ISAIAH 55:8

Thoughts

Be clear minded and self-controlled so that you can pray.

1 PETER 4:7

Whatever is true, whatever is noble, whatever is right, whatever is pure, whatever is lovely, whatever is admirable—if anything is excellent or praise-worthy—think about such things.

PHILIPPIANS 4:8

How precious to me are your thoughts, O God!
    How vast is the sum of them!
Were I to count them,
    they would outnumber the grains of sand.

PSALM 139:17–18

The mind controlled by the sinful nature is death, but the mind controlled by the Spirit is life and peace.

ROMANS 8:6 TNIV

Those who live in accordance with the Spirit have their minds set on what the Spirit desires.

ROMANS 8:5

Time

There will be a time for every activity,
a time for every deed.

ECCLESIASTES 3:17

The wise heart will know the proper time and
procedure.
For there is a proper time and procedure for
every matter.

ECCLESIASTES 8:5–6

My times are in your hands.

PSALM 31:15

A thousand years in your sight, [O LORD,]
are like a day that has just gone by,
or like a watch in the night.

PSALM 90:4

Do not forget this one thing, dear friends: With the
Lord a day is like a thousand years, and a thousand
years are like a day.

2 PETER 3:8

There is a time for everything,
and a season for every activity under heaven.

ECCLESIASTES 3:1

Time

As God's fellow workers we urge you not to receive God's grace in vain. For he says, "In the time of my favor I heard you, and in the day of salvation I helped you." I tell you, now is the time of God's favor, now is the day of salvation.

2 CORINTHIANS 6:1–2

I know that everything God does will endure forever; nothing can be added to it and nothing taken from it. God does it so that men will revere him.

ECCLESIASTES 3:14

You see, at just the right time, when we were still powerless, Christ died for the ungodly.

ROMANS 5:6

[God] has made everything beautiful in its time. He has also set eternity in the hearts of men; yet they cannot fathom what God has done from beginning to end.

ECCLESIASTES 3:11

Trials

The Lord knows how to rescue the godly from trials.

2 PETER 2:9 TNIV

Do not be surprised at the painful trial you are suffering, as though something strange were happening to you. But rejoice that you participate in the sufferings of Christ, so that you may be overjoyed when his glory is revealed. If you are insulted because of the name of Christ, you are blessed, for the Spirit of glory and of God rests on you.

1 PETER 4:12–14

When you are in distress and all these things have happened to you, then in later days you will return to the LORD your God and obey him. For the LORD your God is a merciful God; he will not abandon or destroy you or forget the covenant with your forefathers, which he confirmed to them by oath.

DEUTERONOMY 4:30–31

No temptation has seized you except what is common to man. And God is faithful; he will not let you be tempted beyond what you can bear. But when you are tempted, he will also provide a way out so that you can stand up under it.

1 CORINTHIANS 10:13

Trials

Consider it pure joy ... whenever you face trials of many kinds, because you know that the testing of your faith develops perseverance.

JAMES 1:2

The God of all grace, who called you to his eternal glory in Christ, after you have suffered a little while, will himself restore you and make you strong, firm, and steadfast.

1 PETER 5:10

I consider that our present sufferings are not worth comparing with the glory that will be revealed in us.

ROMANS 8:18

Blessed are those who persevere under trial, because when they have stood the test, they will receive the crown of life that God has promised to those who love him.

JAMES 1:12 TNIV

Trouble

"Because he loves me," says the LORD, "I will
rescue him;
I will protect him, for he acknowledges my name.
He will call upon me, and I will answer him;
I will be with him in trouble,
I will deliver him and honor him."

PSALM 91:14–15

Though I walk in the midst of trouble,
you preserve my life;
you stretch out your hand against the anger of
my foes,
with your right hand you save me.

PSALM 138:7

Jesus said, "In this world you will have trouble. But
take heart! I have overcome the world."

JOHN 16:33

*Our light and momentary troubles are
achieving for us an eternal glory that far
outweighs them all.*

2 CORINTHIANS 4:17

Trouble

Jesus said, "Do not let your hearts be troubled.
Trust in God; trust also in me."

JOHN 14:1

You are my hiding place;
    you will protect me from trouble
    and surround me with songs of deliverance.

PSALM 32:7

The LORD is a refuge for the oppressed,
a stronghold in times of trouble.

PSALM 9:9

Praise be to the God and Father of our LORD Jesus
Christ, the Father of compassion and the God of all
comfort, who comforts us in all our troubles, so that
we can comfort those in any trouble with the
comfort we ourselves have received from God.

2 CORINTHIANS 1:3–4

The righteous may have many troubles,
    but the LORD delivers them from them all.

PSALM 34:19 TNIV

Trust

Those who trust in the LORD are like Mount Zion,
   which cannot be shaken but endures forever.
As the mountains surround Jerusalem,
   so the LORD surrounds his people
   both now and forevermore.

PSALM 125:1–2

Trust in the LORD and do good;
   dwell in the land and enjoy
      safe pasture.

PSALM 37:3

Trust in the LORD forever,
   for the LORD, the LORD, is the Rock eternal.

ISAIAH 26:4

Blessed are those
   who make the LORD their trust,
who do not look to the proud,
   to those who turn aside to false gods.

PSALM 40:4 TNIV

Anyone who believes in [Christ] will
never be put to shame.

ROMANS 10:11

Trust

Blessed are those who trust in the LORD,
    whose confidence is in him.
They will be like a tree planted by the water
    that sends out its roots by the stream.
It does not fear when heat comes;
    its leaves are always green.
It has no worries in a year of drought
    and never fails to bear fruit.

JEREMIAH 17:7–8 TNIV

Trust in the LORD with all your heart
    and lean not on your own understanding;
in all your ways acknowledge him,
    and he will make your paths straight.

PROVERBS 3:5–6

He who trusts in the LORD will prosper.

PROVERBS 28:25

May the God of hope fill you with all joy and peace
as you trust in him, so that you may overflow with
hope by the power of the Holy Spirit.

ROMANS 15:13

Trust

To fear anyone will prove to be a snare,
    but whoever trusts in the LORD is kept safe.

PROVERBS 29:25 TNIV

Some trust in chariots and some in horses,
    but we trust in the name of the LORD our God.
They are brought to their knees and fall,
    but we rise up and stand firm.

PSALM 20:7–8

Whoever dwells in the shelter of the Most High
    will rest in the shadow of the Almighty.
They say of the LORD, "He is my refuge and
        my fortress,
    my God, in whom I trust."

PSALM 91:1–2 TNIV

Many are the woes of the wicked,
    but the LORD's unfailing love
    surrounds those who trust in him.

PSALM 32:10 TNIV

Trust

Those who give heed to instruction prosper,
  and blessed are those who trust in the LORD.

PROVERBS 16:20 TNIV

It is better to take refuge in the LORD
  than to trust in human beings.
It is better to take refuge in the LORD
  than to trust in princes.

PSALM 118:8–9 TNIV

Those who know your name will trust in you,
  for you, LORD, have never forsaken those who
    seek you.

PSALM 9:10

Truth

Jesus answered, "I am the way and the truth and the life. No one comes to the Father except through me."

JOHN 14:6

Those whose walk is blameless,
    who do what is righteous,
    who speak the truth from their hearts. . . .
Whoever does these things
    will never be shaken.

PSALM 15:2, 5 TNIV

All your words are true;
    all your righteous laws are eternal.

PSALM 119:160

Buy the truth and do not sell it;
    get wisdom, discipline and understanding.

PROVERBS 23:23

Jesus said, "If you hold to my teaching, you are really my disciples. Then you will know the truth, and the truth will set you free."

JOHN 8:31–32

Truth

We know that we are children of God, and that the whole world is under the control of the evil one. We know also that the Son of God has come and has given us understanding, so that we may know him who is true. And we are in him who is true—even in his Son Jesus Christ. He is the true God and eternal life.

1 JOHN 5:19–20

Jesus answered, "For this I came into the world, to testify to the truth. Everyone on the side of truth listens to me."

JOHN 18:37

Jesus said, "I have much more to say to you, more than you can now bear. But when he, the Spirit of truth, comes, he will guide you into all truth. He will not speak on his own; he will speak only what he hears, and he will tell you what is yet to come."

JOHN 16:12–13

Understanding

Those who cherish understanding will soon prosper.

PROVERBS 19:8 TNIV

Blessed are those who find wisdom,
    those who gain understanding,
for she is more profitable than silver
    and yields better returns than gold.
She is more precious than rubies;
    nothing you desire can compare with her.
Long life is in her right hand;
    in her left hand are riches and honor.
Her ways are pleasant ways,
    and all her paths are peace.
She is a tree of life to those who take hold of her;
    those who hold her fast will be blessed.

PROVERBS 3:13–18 TNIV

Who is wise and understanding among you? Let him show it by his good life, by deeds done in the humility that comes from wisdom.

JAMES 3:13

Understanding

My purpose is that they may be encouraged in heart and united in love, so that they may have the full riches of complete understanding, in order that they may know the mystery of God, namely, Christ, in whom are hidden all the treasures of wisdom and knowledge.

COLOSSIANS 2:2–3

I have more understanding than the elders,
> for I obey your precepts.
I gain understanding from your precepts.

PSALM 119:100, 104

It is the spirit in mortals,
> *the breath of the Almighty, that gives*
> *them understanding.*

JOB 32:8 TNIV

Though it cost all you have, get understanding.
Esteem her, and she will exalt you;
> embrace her, and she will honor you.
She will set a garland of grace on your head
> and present you with a crown of splendor.

PROVERBS 4:7–9

Unity

May the God who gives endurance and encouragement give you a spirit of unity among yourselves as you follow Christ Jesus.

ROMANS 15:5

There is neither Jew nor Greek, slave nor free, male nor female, for you are all one in Christ Jesus.

GALATIANS 3:28

We were all baptized by one Spirit into one body— whether Jews or Greeks, slave or free—and we were all given the one Spirit to drink.

1 CORINTHIANS 12:13

As far as it depends on you, live at peace with everyone.

ROMANS 12:18

There is one body and one Spirit—just as you were called to one hope when you were called—one Lord, one faith, one baptism; one God and Father of all, who is over all and through all and in all.

EPHESIANS 4:4–6

Unity

Agree with one another so that there may be no divisions among you.

1 CORINTHIANS 1:10

Jesus said, "I pray also for those who will believe in me.... May they be brought to complete unity to let the world know that you sent me."

JOHN 17:20–23

Make every effort to keep the unity of the Spirit.

EPHESIANS 4:3

Live in harmony with one another.

ROMANS 12:16

How good and pleasant it is
　　when God's people live together in unity!

PSALM 133:1 TNIV

Be like-minded, be sympathetic, love one another, be compassionate and humble.

1 PETER 3:8 TNIV

Unselfishness

A generous person will prosper;
  whoever refreshes others will be refreshed.

PROVERBS 11:25 TNIV

If you harbor bitter envy and selfish ambition in your hearts, do not boast about it or deny the truth. Such "wisdom" does not come down from heaven but is earthly, unspiritual, of the devil. For where you have envy and selfish ambition, there you find disorder and every evil practice. But the wisdom that comes from above is first of all pure; then peace-loving, considerate, submissive, full of mercy and good fruit, impartial and sincere. Peacemakers who sow in peace raise a harvest of righteousness.

JAMES 3:14–18

Do nothing out of selfish ambition or vain conceit, but in humility consider others better than yourselves. Each of you should look not only to your own interests, but also to the interests of others.

PHILIPPIANS 2:3–4

Jesus said, "Watch out! Be on your guard against all kinds of greed; life does not consist in an abundance of possessions."

LUKE 12:15 TNIV

Unselfishness

Those who are kind to the poor lend to the LORD,
and he will reward them for what they
have done.

PROVERBS 19:17 TNIV

*Jesus said, "Give to the one who asks
you, and do not turn away from the one
who wants to borrow from you."*

MATTHEW 5:42

Turn my heart toward your statutes
and not toward selfish gain.
Turn my eyes away from worthless things;
preserve my life according to your word.

PSALM 119:36–37

Love is patient, love is kind. It does not envy, it
does not boast, it is not proud. It is not rude, it is
not self-seeking, it is not easily angered, it keeps no
record of wrongs.

1 CORINTHIANS 13:4–5

Values

Be shepherds of God's flock that is under your care, serving as overseers—not because you must, but because you are willing, as God wants you to be; not greedy for money, but eager to serve; not lording it over those entrusted to you, but being examples to the flock.

1 PETER 5:2–3

Be careful, and watch yourselves closely so that you do not forget the things your eyes have seen or let them slip from your heart as long as you live. Teach them to your children and to their children after them.

DEUTERONOMY 4:9

Be careful that you do not forget the LORD your God, failing to observe his commands, his laws and his decrees. . . . Otherwise, when you eat and are satisfied, when you build fine houses and settle down, and when your herds and flocks grow large and your silver and gold increase and all you have is multiplied, then your heart will become proud and you will forget the LORD your God.

DEUTERONOMY 8:11–14

Values

Jesus said, "Do to others as you would have them do to you."

LUKE 6:31

Whatever is true, whatever is noble, whatever is right, whatever is pure, whatever is lovely, whatever is admirable—if anything is excellent or praiseworthy—think about such things.

PHILIPPIANS 4:8

Who may ascend the mountain of the LORD?
   Who may stand in his holy place?
Those who have clean hands and a pure heart,
   who do not put their trust in an idol
   or swear by a false god.
They will receive blessing from the LORD
   and vindication from God their Savior.

PSALM 24:3–5 TNIV

Victory

[God] holds victory in store for the upright.

PROVERBS 2:7

There is no wisdom, no insight, no plan
   that can succeed against the LORD.
The horse is made ready for the day of battle,
   but victory rests with the LORD.

PROVERBS 21:30–31

With God we will gain the victory,
   and he will trample down our enemies.

PSALM 60:12

Jesus said, "In this world you will have trouble. But take heart! I have overcome the world."

JOHN 16:33

His commands are not burdensome, for everyone
born of God overcomes the world. This is the victory
that has overcome the world, even our faith. Who is
it that overcomes the world? Only he who believes
that Jesus is the Son of God.

1 JOHN 5:3–5

Victory

Thanks be to God, who always leads us in triumphal procession in Christ.

2 CORINTHIANS 2:14

In all these things we are more than conquerors through him who loved us.

ROMANS 8:37

The LORD your God is the one who goes with you to fight for you against your enemies to give you victory.

DEUTERONOMY 20:4

We will not all sleep, but we will all be changed—in a flash, in the twinkling of an eye, at the last trumpet. For the trumpet will sound, the dead will be raised imperishable, and we will be changed.... Then the saying that is written will come true: "Death has been swallowed up in victory." ... Thanks be to God! He gives us the victory through our Lord Jesus Christ.

1 CORINTHIANS 15:51–52, 54, 57

Wisdom

If you accept my words
    and store up my commands within you,
turning your ear to wisdom
    and applying your heart to understanding,
and if you call out for insight
    and cry aloud for understanding,
and if you look for it as for silver
    and search for it as for hidden treasure,
then you will understand the fear of the LORD
    and find the knowledge of God.

PROVERBS 2:1–5

The fear of the LORD is the beginning of wisdom;
    all who follow his precepts have good
        understanding.
To him belongs eternal praise.

PSALM 111:10

Wisdom is sweet to your soul;
    if you find it, there is a future hope for you,
    and your hope will not be cut off.

PROVERBS 24:14

Do not forsake wisdom, and she will protect you;
    love her, and she will watch over you.
Wisdom is supreme; therefore get wisdom.

PROVERBS 4:6

Wisdom

If any of you lacks wisdom, he should ask God, who gives generously to all without finding fault, and it will be given to him.

JAMES 1:5

"I guide you in the way of wisdom
  and lead you along straight paths.
When you walk, your steps will not be hampered;
  when you run, you will not stumble,"
    says the LORD.

PROVERBS 4:11–12

The wisdom that comes from heaven is first of all pure; then peace-loving, considerate, submissive, full of mercy and good fruit, impartial and sincere.

JAMES 3:17

Wisdom, like an inheritance, is a good thing and benefits those who see the sun.

ECCLESIASTES 7:11

Work

Whatever you do, work at it with all your heart, as working for the Lord, not for human masters, since you know that you will receive an inheritance from the Lord as a reward.

COLOSSIANS 3:23–24 TNIV

Diligent hands will rule.

PROVERBS 12:24

Don't you know that those who work in the temple get their food from the temple, and those who serve at the altar share in what is offered on the altar? In the same way, the Lord has commanded that those who preach the gospel should receive their living from the gospel.

1 CORINTHIANS 9:13–14

The sluggard craves and gets nothing,
    but the desires of the diligent are fully satisfied.

PROVERBS 13:4

*Lazy hands make for poverty,
    but diligent hands bring wealth.*

PROVERBS 10:4 TNIV

Work

All hard work brings a profit.

PROVERBS 14:23

God is not unjust; he will not forget your work and the love you have shown him as you have helped his people and continue to help them.

HEBREWS 6:10

Stand firm. Let nothing move you. Always give yourselves fully to the work of the Lord, because you know that your labor in the Lord is not in vain.

1 CORINTHIANS 15:58

From the fruit of their lips people are filled with
      good things,
    and the work of their hands brings them reward.

PROVERBS 12:14 TNIV

Jesus said, "Do not work for food that spoils, but for food that endures to eternal life, which the Son of Man will give you. On him God the Father has placed his seal of approval."

JOHN 6:27

We want to hear from you. Please send your
comments about this book to us in care of
zreview@zondervan.com. Thank you.